GENES & DISEASE

ALZHEIMER'S DISEASE

GENES & DISEASE

Alzheimer's Disease

Asthma

Cystic Fibrosis

Diabetes

Down Syndrome

Hemophilia

Huntington's Disease

Parkinson's Disease

Sickle Cell Disease

Tay-Sachs Disease

GENES & DISEASE

ALZHEIMER'S DISEASE

Evelyn B. Kelly, Ph.D.

CHELSEA HOUSE
PUBLISHERS
An imprint of Infobase Publishing

Chelsea House
An imprint of Infobase Publishing
132 West 31st Street
New York NY 10001

Library of Congress Cataloging-in-Publication Data

Kelly, Evelyn B.
   Alzheimer's disease / Evelyn B. Kelly.
      p. cm. — (Genes and disease)
   Includes bibliographical references and index.
   ISBN 978-0-7910-9588-1 (hardcover)
   1. Alzheimer's disease. I. Title. II. Series.
   RC523.3.K45 2008
   616.8'31—dc22 2007051319

Chelsea House books are available at special discounts when purchased in bulk quantities for businesses, associations, institutions, or sales promotions. Please call our Special Sales Department in New York at (212) 967-8800 or (800) 322-8755.

You can find Chelsea House on the World Wide Web at
http://www.chelseahouse.com

Text design by Annie O'Donnell
Cover design by Ben Peterson

Printed in the United States of America

Bang NMSG 10 9 8 7 6 5 4 3 2 1

This book is printed on acid-free paper.

All links and Web addresses were checked and verified to be correct at the time of publication. Because of the dynamic nature of the Web, some addresses and links may have changed since publication and may no longer be valid.

CONTENTS

1

ALZHEIMER'S DISEASE: A BRAIN OF CLUMPS AND PLAQUES

"Those men won't talk to me," said 79-year-old Marsha Knight as she came in from her daily walk on the farm. "They would not talk. They just ran away."

Todd, Marsha's son, was puzzled. He knew the workers on his Florida horse farm well, and he knew that there were no men in the area of the field where his mother had been. When Todd went out to check, he found only his thoroughbred horses across the white boarded fence. Marsha thought the horses were men. She has a disease that robs her of her memory for faces and impairs her judgment. The disease is called Alzheimer's disease. The nerve cells in her brain are dying.

Jeannette and Andy Green built their dream home away from the city on a peaceful Florida lake. One afternoon as the sun was setting, Jeannette found Andy in the lake with only his head out of the water. Andy, age 50, has early-onset Alzheimer's disease, which can affect people even in their forties. He does not remember where he is or what he has done. Like other people with Alzheimer's disease, he is prone to wander, especially at sundown.

When Orlon and Susan Lott moved to Florida from New York, they dreamed of a life without shoveling snow. They pictured days of playing golf in their gated community. One day Orlon found his wife's glasses in the refrigerator and her car keys in the sugar bowl. One nippy day, he found her walking the streets of the community barefoot and clad only in her pajama top. Orlon's wife has early-stage Alzheimer's disease.

WHAT IS ALZHEIMER'S DISEASE?

Alzheimer's disease (AD) is a condition in which the brain slowly shrivels and dies. Nerve cells in the brain stop working, and brain signals that are essential for life do not function properly. Although some people believe that **dementia** and decline in the later years are inevitable, **geriatricians**—who study and treat diseases of older adults—strongly disagree. Alzheimer's disease and other dementias are considered illnesses and are not part of normal aging.

Alzheimer's disease starts with mild memory loss. People with AD gradually lose judgment, thinking, and reasoning ability, or **cognition**. Personality and behavior change. The person may become anxious, agitated, and delusional. The progressive loss of intellectual abilities is called **dementia.** As the disease progresses, the individual needs help in all phases of life, including bathing, eating, and using the restroom. Families and friends of people with AD are especially affected. Seeing their loved ones change from the person they once knew to a stranger is emotionally devastating.

Although there is no cure for AD at present, hope is on the horizon. Advances in **molecular biology** and **genetics** are offering insights into causes that could lead to a cure or to preventive measures. Most scientists now agree that AD is a genetic disease. They have located the genes that may cause some kinds of early-onset AD. Researchers throughout the world are working on connections between the environment and genetics in the many types of dementia.

THE BRAIN AND AD

The **nervous system** comprises the brain, spinal cord, and nerves that extend to all parts of the body. A normal brain really is not spectacular to look at. It weighs only about 3 pounds and has the texture of stiff, thick custard. Students looking at it for the first time are often amazed that

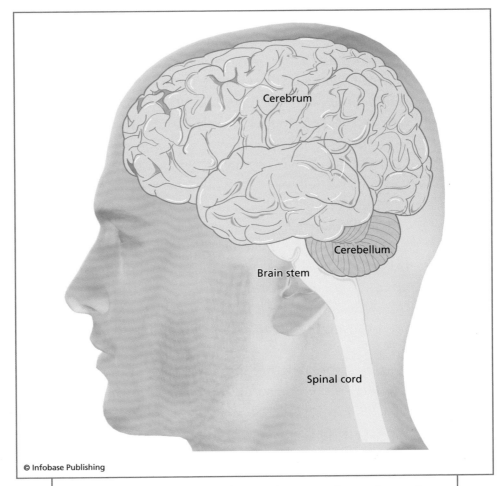

© Infobase Publishing

FIGURE 1.1   The brain has three main parts: the cerebrum, the cerebellum, and the brainstem. The spinal cord relays information between the brain and the rest of the nervous system.

this unimportant looking structure controls all thoughts, movements, and bodily functions.

The brain has three main parts:

◆ **Cerebrum**. The **cerebrum** is the thinking part of the brain. It fills the upper part of the skull and is involved in memory, problem solving, the senses (sight, hearing, touch, etc.), speech, and voluntary movements. The outermost layer of the cerebrum, called the cerebral cortex, has numerous folds and wrinkles. The cortex is where thoughts are generated, memories are stored, and the senses of sight, sound, and smell are processed. AD affects this part of the brain, especially in the early stages of the disease.

◆ Cerebellum. The cerebellum, which looks like a piece of cauliflower, is located below the cerebrum at the back of the head. It controls coordination and balance.

◆ Brainstem. The brainstem sits beneath the cerebrum in front of the cerebellum and connects the upper parts of the brain to the spinal cord. The brainstem controls breathing, heart rate, blood pressure, and other automatic functions.

The basic unit of structure in the nervous system is the **neuron,** or nerve cell. The adult brain has about 100 billion nerve cells, with branches that connect at more than a trillion points. Looking at a picture of neurons and their connections is like looking at a forest of deep underbrush.

Neurons are similar to other body cells in some ways and different in others. They are like all other cells in that they have a **nucleus,** the central part of the cell, which contains

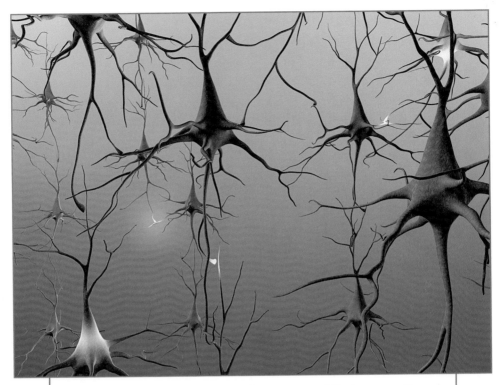

FIGURE 1.2   The arrangement of neurons and their connections in the brain can be likened to a forest of deep underbrush.

the cell's genetic material. The **cytoplasm,** or the part of a cell that surrounds the nucleus, contains other structures called **organelles.** The **cell membrane** surrounds the cytoplasm and nucleus, and controls the movement of materials into and out of the cell.

Neurons are different from other cells in that they have specialized extensions called dendrites and axons. The **dendrites,** which look like tree branches, extend out from the cell body. The **cell body** is an enlarged part of the neuron that contains the nucleus and various cell organelles. A single, long **axon** extends from the end of the neuron away from the dendrites. Information is transmitted from one neuron to the next in the form of impulses, which are small areas of electrical charge and chemical data that travel along the cell membranes of neurons. Impulses are transmitted from the axon of one neuron to the dendrites of the next. They travel down the dendrites to the cell body and then down the axon to specialized axon endings.

Neurons communicate with each other both chemically and electrically. They do not touch. Messages are carried between neurons by means of special chemicals called **neurotransmitters** that are released at the axon endings. Scientists have found a number of different neurotransmitters, which function in different parts of the nervous system.

Alzheimer's disease disrupts several functions of the brain. It affects both the impulses as they travel along the neurons and the activity of neurotransmitters. Neurons are the chief type of cells that AD destroys.

In time, AD leads to nerve and tissue loss throughout the brain. Images of the brain taken using magnetic resonance imaging and other noninvasive techniques show how the brain shrinks in an individual with advanced AD. The areas of the brain most affected by AD, and their corresponding symptoms, include:

- The cerebral cortex. The thought, planning, and memory part of the brain forms clumps and tangled neurons.
- The **hippocampus**. This major structure, which plays an important role in forming memories, shrinks like a dried-up pea.
- **Ventricles**. Ventricles, or fluid-filled cavities in the brain, get larger.

TANGLED THREADS

When scientists look at slides of brain tissue from a person with AD, they see a mass of tangled, mixed-up neurons. These masses are called **neurofibrillary tangles (NFTS)**. Clumps of **plaque,** or abnormal protein bits, are lodged between neurons. Although researchers are not sure what causes the death of the brain cells, plaques and tangles are two strong suspects.

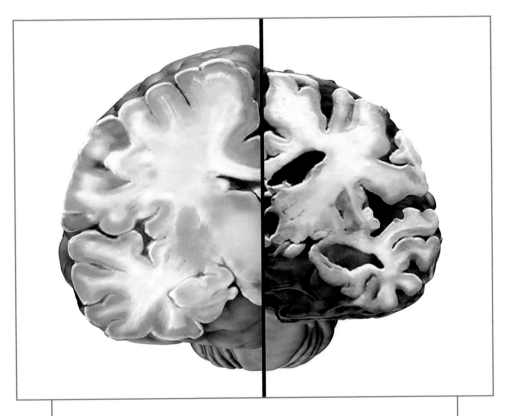

FIGURE 1.3 This photo shows a crosswise "slice" through the brain. On the left is a healthy brain; on the right, one with advanced Alzheimer's disease. In the Alzheimer's brain, the cerebral cortex has shriveled and the ventricles (fluid-filled spaces) have grown larger.

Doctors know how the plaques and tangles will spread. The process is quite predictable, but the rate varies from person to person. The average person with AD lives about 8 years, but some may live as long as 20 years with the disease.

TYPES OF AD

There are three basic types of Alzheimer's disease:

- ◆ **Early-onset AD** is a rare form of the disease that afflicts people younger than 65. Less than 10% of people with AD have this type. Memory loss, behavior changes, and premature aging characterize this type.
- ◆ **Late-onset AD,** the most common form, accounts for about 90% of cases and usually occurs after age 65. Geneticists are working hard to make the

HIPPOCAMPUS: A CURVED HORSE

The hippocampus is a tiny structure located deep in the brain under the temporal lobe. In 1584, when the Italian anatomist Guilio Aranzi first dissected the brain, he noted a structure on either side that looked like a seahorse, the animal named after the mythological curved horses that drove the chariot of Poseidon, or Neptune, the sea god. Aranzi called the structure the hippocampus. *Hippos* is the Greek word meaning "horse" and *kampi* is a Greek word meaning "curved."

Many experiments have shown that the hippocampus is critical to learning and memory. In some circles, it is thought to be the memory's control center. In AD, the hippocampus is one of the first regions to suffer damage.

connection between genes and AD. There are several suspect genes.

◆ **Familial Alzheimer's disease (FAD)**. This form is inherited. In affected families, at least two generations have had the condition. FAD is rare and accounts for less than 1% of all cases of AD. People may display symptoms of FAD as early as age 40.

WHO GETS AD?

According to the Alzheimer's Association, about 4.5 million Americans have AD. It is estimated that 18 million people worldwide suffer from the effects of this disease. In a study of a community of older persons, an estimated 13% over age 65 had probable AD; nearly half of those over age 85 had the disease. Its prevalence is associated with age. As the population of older adults increases, the number of people with AD will also increase. The Alzheimer's Association projects the number of people who will have AD in the twenty-first century will rise from 4.5 million in 2000 to 5.62 million in 2020 to 15 million in 2050.

AD ranks seventh in the cause of death among people of all ages. In 2007, 71,696 death certificates listed the cause of death as Alzheimer's. Likewise, AD is one of the most expensive diseases facing the nation. Including medical and nursing home care, social services, and lost productivity, the annual cost of AD to the nation is estimated at $90 billion. Advances in understanding the genetics and molecular biology of AD are shedding light on the basic disease processes, and scientists are working toward a cure.

This book is an exploration of Alzheimer's disease. It will present the current knowledge of the disease and the discoveries that form the basis of hope for treatment and eventual cure. This book includes a brief history of the disease. Chapter 2 tells the story of how Dr. Alois Alzheimer discovered the disease and how it was treated in the past. Chapter 3 describes the symptoms and diagnosis of the

DISEASES THAT ACT LIKE AD

Although AD is the most common cause of dementia, several other conditions can cause similar symptoms.

- Vascular dementia: a condition in which the blood supply to the brain is inadequate.
- Parkinson's disease: a disease resulting in tremors and loss of muscle control; dementia may occur in later stages.
- Lewy body disease: a disease with symptoms of both Parkinson's and Alzheimer's diseases.
- Creutzfeldt-Jakob disease (CJD): a rare fatal disease caused by infection; related to mad cow disease.
- Pick's disease: a rare brain disease that affects the front parts of the brain.
- Huntington's disease: a hereditary disorder character-ized by irregular movement of arms and limbs and a decline in reasoning and thinking ability.
- Normal pressure hydrocephalus: a rare disease caused by obstruction of the flow of spinal fluid.
- Certain nutritional deficiencies, such as vitamin B12 and folate deficiencies, may cause dementia.
- Head injury.
- Certain kidney, liver, and lung diseases.
- Toxic reactions from overuse of drugs and alcohol.

Unlike AD, some of these conditions can be treated. For example, vitamin B12 can be given to people with a deficiency of that vitamin.

disease. In Chapter 4, an exploration of fundamental genetics and the Human Genome Project form the basis for understanding the genetics of the disease. Chapters 5, 6, and 7 present the development of DNA technology, the search for faulty genes, and current therapies. Chapter 8 discusses future treatments. The final chapter considers ethical concerns of treating or preventing genetic diseases and examines research issues, such as informed consent.

NEW NAME, OLD DISEASE

Alzheimer's disease is not new to the world. The behavior of people with dementia has been well known for centuries. The Greek philosopher Plato (429–348 B.C.) believed that a person in a state of madness or under the influence of old age was not responsible for his crimes. Plato did not blame problems of judgment on the brain, but on spiritual weakness. He also recognized, however, that some older people were perfectly rational and that decline was not a normal part of aging.

Cicero (106–43 B.C.), a Roman statesman and orator, stated that what he termed "senile folly," or foolishness, is not characteristic of all old men, but of only a few. He maintained that older men were wiser than younger men. He did not believe that cognitive decline was a part of aging.

A change in the attitude toward dementia and old age came with the Roman physician Galen (A.D. 130–200). Studying the bodies and brains of animals, Galen refined the Greek idea that a balance of bodily "humors" regulated health. He believed that evaporation of body heat and moisture caused aging, which was the drying out and shriveling up of the body. On Galen's authority, medical writers distinguished four main categories of insanity: frenzy, mania, melancholy, and fatuity. These conditions were believed to be caused when the humors were out of balance. People with AD may show each of these symptoms at one stage of the disease or another. Galen's teachings about the humors influenced thought about the body for more than 1,000 years.

Several kinds of "treatments" were used during this thousand-year period. Priests exorcised, or cast out, the demons or devils that were thought to afflict people who exhibited bizarre behavior. Special saints and shrines emerged to treat madness. For example, a shrine of St. Dymphna, the patron saint of the mentally ill, was built in the thirteenth century in Gheel, Belgium, and is still in existence today. This shrine initially housed the mentally ill. When there were more people than the shrine could hold, people in the village took them in, developing a unique type of community care. The standard method used to balance the humors was opening a **vein** and bleeding the person. Many towns, however, put the mentally ill in asylums, where they were often chained or restrained. Other towns set aside special rooms in their hospitals. Monasteries also cared for the mentally ill. In 1403, St. Mary of Bethlehem in London took in six men "deprived of reason"; this madhouse

HUMORAL MEDICINE

Many ancient systems of medicine—including Chinese, Indian, Greek, and Roman—believed in some form of humors. The idea of humors basically held that there were four humors, or bodily fluids—blood, phlegm, yellow bile, and black bile. A person was healthy when the humors were in balance; illness resulted when the humors were out of balance. The belief in humors was part of medical thinking that continued into the nineteenth century.

eventually became the notorious Bedlam, a place of horrors and cruelty.

During the Middle Ages, people did not worry about the diseases of older people. The average life expectancy was about 30 years. People were more concerned about day-to-day survival. People seldom lived into their sixties, and people in their eighties were a rarity. Those who did live to old age and did not have families to support them were often isolated in prisons or placed in shackles. William Shakespeare (1564–1616), in his comedy *As You Like It*, described seven stages of man. The final stage is old age, in which man is "sans teeth, sans eyes, sans taste, sans everything." (*Sans* is a French word that means "without.")

THE EIGHTEENTH CENTURY: THE AGE OF ENLIGHTMENT

During the Age of Enlightenment, a time when people started applying scientific principles to solve unanswered mysteries, some thinkers began to view diseases and their causes differently. A French doctor—Philippe Pinel (1745–1826)—believed that mental illness had a cause and a cure. Pinel was the first to use the term *dementia*, meaning incoherence of the mental faculties. At the turn of the nineteenth century, Pinel changed the asylum model in France by introducing the idea of humane treatment for the mentally ill. Instead of isolating and chaining people with dementia, he proposed that doctors should interact with patients to treat them.

THE NINETEENTH CENTURY

Despite advances made by Pinel and his contemporaries, use of restraints never completely disappeared during the nineteenth century. The debate about how to treat the

BEDLAM

Bedlam now refers to chaos and disorder. Originally, however, it was the name of an asylum for mental patients where terrible conditions prevailed for hundreds of years. Violent or dangerous patients were chained to the floor or wall. Others roamed around. There was no heat or sanitation. In the eighteenth century, people would go to Bedlam for entertainment to see the lunatics. For one penny, they could view the "freak show." The visitors brought long sticks to poke at the inmates, encouraging them to fight each other. Sometimes the nonviolent inmates were permitted to go outside and beg. They wore a tin plate strapped to an arm to show they were beggars of Bedlam.

mentally ill raged. A myth emerged that the mentally ill did not have normal senses, such as the ability to detect heat and cold. Such myths led to abuse and terrible conditions within the asylums.

The belief that decline is inevitable as a person ages emerged strongly during the nineteenth century. The American physician George Beard believed that there was a relationship between age and creativity. In his study—which was certainly not scientific—he found that 70% of a person's creative work was done by the age of 45, and 80% by age 50. He believed that intellectual and moral decline were part of aging. His opinion was not unique; it was already entrenched in the minds of the greater population. The word *senile*, which once simply meant old, was redefined in the nineteenth century to mean an inevitable decline as a person reaches old age. Although no scientific basis supports this belief, it is still widely held.

Enter Alois Alzheimer

The second half of the nineteenth century marked a period of great change in the field of medicine. Amazing developments had changed science. The discovery of microbes led to the idea, radical at that time, that germs cause disease. Improved microscopes allowed for the development of the field of microbiology.

Alois Alzheimer was born on June 14, 1864, in Markbreit, Germany. His family had a tradition of its members devoting themselves to serving humanity, and many members had become teachers and priests. He saw the medical profession as a meaningful way to combine his interest in science with service to humanity.

Berlin at the time was home to many famous doctors. In Berlin, Alzheimer heard of John Connolly, a British doctor who had devised new treatments for mental illness. Connolly's nonrestraint principle of treating the insane without using chains and shackles fascinated him. After attending several schools for training, Alzheimer graduated with an interest in the new field of clinical psychotherapy, which combined psychiatry and microscopic tissue research.

Psychiatrists of the time were called *Irrenärtze*, which literally means "looney doctors"; they were also referred to as "alienists." After graduating in 1888, Alzheimer became an intern at the Municipal Asylum for the Insane and Epileptic in Frankfurt-am-Main in Germany. Doctors there had sought to implement new techniques, such as nonrestraint and bath therapy. They believed that mental illnesses were brain illnesses rather than a result of spiritual or personal weakness.

It was a gloomy day in November 1901 that changed Alzheimer's life and the outlook of the medical profession toward mental illness. Alzheimer glanced at the file of

Auguste D., a 51-year-old woman, and could not put it down. These files are documented in his biography, *Alzheimer: The Life of a Physician and the Career of a Disease.* Auguste had just finished eating cauliflower and pork for lunch. When he asked her what she had eaten, she answered, "Spinach and first I eat the potatoes and then the horseradish." He asked her to write her name; she wrote "Mrs." and forgot the rest. He knew that he had an unusual patient.

Auguste's behavior with other patients was also a problem. She was constantly fearful and walked around saying, "I won't let myself be cut." Thinking she was blind, she stumbled about the room groping faces of other patients. They slapped her. During the night, she woke up other patients. She finally had to be placed in an isolation room. With passing years, she became more hostile, screaming when anyone wanted to examine her. She would scream for hours on end. Alzheimer referred to her conditions as presenile dementia.

Alzheimer left Frankfurt and eventually ended up working at an asylum in Munich. He made friends with the renowned psychiatrist Emil Kraepelin. On April 9, 1906, an intern from Frankfurt called to tell him that Auguste had died. Alzheimer immediately requested her files and her brain so he could examine it under the microscope. He studied the brain carefully and noted that deterioration of the 56-year-old woman's brain was far more advanced than that of a 70- or 80-year-old. What he saw next under the microscope was more amazing: a tangle of neurons and deposits distributed throughout the brain. At Kraepelin's suggestion, he presented his findings at a scientific meeting in 1906, and the results were published in 1907.

Alzheimer began studying the brains of other patients. In March 1907, a new patient, Mrs. B.A., age 65, arrived under Alzheimer's observation. She had a zombie-like appearance

FIGURE 2.1 Alois Alzheimer was a German psychiatrist who is credited with identifying the first published case of "presenile dementia," which later became known as Alzheimer's disease.

and repeated a few childish-sounding phrases, incapable of further speech. When she died two weeks later, he was able to dissect her brain. He found the same plaques and tangles that he had first discovered on the brain of Auguste D. Another person, a clerk of the court, was admitted with suspected dementia. In his hospital room, he held court all by himself and talked to former lovers (who were not there). Another man, a basket maker, was admitted at the age of 45. His memory loss had progressed for five years; he could not remember how to go to the bathroom and relieved himself in the room or in his pants. Alzheimer now had four cases for study. When he studied the brains during **autopsy**, he found the same plaques and tangles in each of them.

The next event permanently associated the name of Alzheimer with the disease. Kraepelin revised a version of his famous textbook on psychiatry in which he included "Alzheimer's disease," which was defined as dementia afflicting those younger than 60. (Later scientists would discover these same plaques and tangles in people older than 60.) Kraepelin's act of naming the disease after Alzheimer gave credit to the scientist who made the startling connection

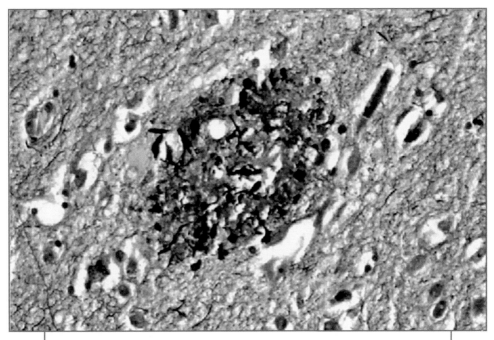

FIGURE 2.2 This photograph shows the deposits, or plaques, characteristic of Alzheimer's disease.

between plaques and tangles in the brain and dementia. Alzheimer died in 1915 at age 51 from kidney failure.

THE TWENTIETH CENTURY

During the first half of the twentieth century, **neurology**, the study of the nervous system and its diseases, progressed. Study of diseases of the heart and **arteries** led most doctors to conclude that dementia was caused by hardening and thickening of the artery walls, causing reduced blood flow to the brain. With the advance of medicine and such new tools as the electron microscope, researchers were able to look at the brain in a new light. With the advent of antibiotics and vaccination, life expectancy increased. Many people were living much longer. The effects of an aging population hit home in the years between 1940 and 1960, so much so that Congress passed a bill to create **Medicare**, a federal health insurance program for people 65 and older.

Alzheimer's Disease Goes Public

At the beginning of the 1970s, Alzheimer's disease was basically unknown to the general public. During that decade, two movements in the United States helped to change the situation. In 1974, Congress created the **National Institute on Aging (NIA).** The institute was designed to carry on biomedical, social, and behavioral research on aging. Robert Butler, head of the NIA, convinced the staff to focus on one disease to be the main priority of the new institute. The disease they chose was Alzheimer's disease.

The second force behind greater public recognition of Alzheimer's disease came with the creation of an advocacy group called the Alzheimer's Association. Several representatives from support groups for families affected by AD came together to discuss the need for an official group that would advocate for people with Alzheimer's and their families at a national level. They held the first board meeting of the Alzheimer's Disease and Related Disorders Association (ADRDA) in 1979. Then, an amazing letter to the newspaper columnist Dear Abby (Abigail Van Buren) made a strong impact. The letter writer told of her difficulty in dealing with a relative with dementia. Abby referred the writer to ADRDA. Over the next few weeks, the new organization received more than 25,000 requests for information. ADRDA later became the Alzheimer's Association.

It took two celebrities with Alzheimer's disease, however, to engage the interest of the public. Rita Hayworth was a

FIGURE 2.3   Actress Rita Hayworth suffered from an extremely early onset of Alzheimer's disease, which was not diagnosed until 1980. The title role in the film *Gilda* (1946) was perhaps her most famous.

FIGURE 2.4 President Ronald Reagan, whose first job was as a radio announcer for Chicago Cubs baseball games, left office in 1989 and disclosed he had been diagnosed with Alzheimer's disease in 1994.

captivating redhead who was known as the "love goddess" in the 1940s. Her movies were great hits, and she had a large following. In the 1960s, however, Hayworth began to change. She was afraid to go into corners of her home by herself, cried out for no apparent reason, and hurled unfair accusations at others. She soon forgot what she had to say, and her films had to be shot line for line. She wandered aimlessly through the streets of Beverly Hills looking like a homeless drifter. Yasmin Khan, Hayworth's daughter from her third marriage, placed her in front of the mirror and tried to show her who she was: "See, that's you, Rita Hayworth." She only stared back.

Yasmin, however, did not stop here. She wrote an appeal to President Ronald Reagan about the terrible effects of this disease and urged him to devote more federal funds for study. He answered her letter, and in the fiscal year of 1984, funds were increased from $17 million to $25 million.

The last years of Hayworth's life were similar to those of Auguste D., whom Dr. Alzheimer had treated in 1901. When Hayworth died in 1987, Yasmin told the doctors that she wanted the world to know about Alzheimer's disease and gave permission to give out her mother's medical records. Thus, the death of the famous actress made Alzheimer's disease known throughout the world.

Seven years later, President Reagan's acknowledgement of his own diagnosis of Alzheimer's disease had a similarly positive impact on public awareness. In a handwritten letter to the public in 1994, he announced, "I have recently been told that I am one of the millions of Americans who will be afflicted with Alzheimer's disease." His note concluded, "I now begin the journey that will lead me into the sunset of my life." The next year, an article in the *Boston Globe* reported that Reagan had attended a dinner at a restaurant in Los Angeles. When he left, the other diners began to applaud him as Mr. President. He did not understand why they were clapping; he did not remember being president. Ronald Reagan died in 2004.

Alzheimer's disease is a serious progressive disease that robs people of their minds and memories. Chapter 3 looks in detail at the symptoms and behaviors associated with Alzheimer's disease.

AD—SYMPTOMS
AND BEHAVIOR

Suppose a test had these three questions or tasks:

1. Add two plus three.
2. Count backward beginning with 10.
3. What day of the week is it?

This test is a piece of cake. It would be easy for most people to pass. A person in the middle stage of Alzheimer's disease, however, would not be able to answer questions from this simple and quick test used for diagnosis of Alzheimer's disease.

SAILING INTO DARKNESS

Iris Murdoch (1919–1999) was a brilliant writer and professor at Oxford University in Great Britain. She wrote fantasy novels and psychological thrillers, sometimes composing entire books in her mind. She was such a perfectionist that she would not let editors change one word of her writing. Then, suddenly, her writing changed. She began to make many errors and even repeated long blocks of text several times. One day she said to her husband, John Bayley, that she felt she was "sailing into the darkness." Indeed, AD had long been at work in her brain by that point. In just a hand-ful of years, Iris changed from brilliant intellect to "a very nice three-year-old," according to Bayley. He captured her descent into darkness in a book called *Elegy for Iris*, which was later made into the movie *Iris*.

SYMPTOMS IN THREE STAGES

How do people decide that their loved ones have a physical or mental disease? One must look at symptoms. Some dis-eases with tell-tale symptoms, such as measles, are simple to diagnose. Mental diseases, such as depression, have obvious symptoms of sadness and withdrawal from the world. Alzheimer's disease and "sailing into the darkness," however, are not easy to diagnose, especially in early stages. Doctors must rely on certain signs and behaviors for clues.

In people with AD, changes in the brain may begin 10 to 20 years before noticeable symptoms appear. The area of the brain thought to control memory, the hippocampus, may be the first to shrink. How can doctors diagnose the disease if they cannot look into the living brain? Dr. Barry Reisberg of New York University has developed a scale called the Functional Assessment Staging Test (FAST). The FAST scale divides the progression of Alzheimer's into three stages based on symptoms and behavior. Over time, as new symptoms appear, the disease progresses through these stages. According to the FAST scale, the three stages are mild, moderate, and severe.

Mild Alzheimer's Disease

The body of the person in the mild stage of AD often appears healthy, but he or she may begin having trouble making sense of the world around them. This confusion at first may appear normal. Even healthy adults have times when they have trouble understanding their world. Determining what is AD and what is normal aging may be critical at this point. The person assessing symptoms must know how to distinguish between the signs of normal aging and the signs of AD.

AGING ISN'T JUST YEARS: PROGERIA

Crowds ebbed and flowed around what looked like two bald, shriveled old men wearing Mickey Mouse caps and licking ice cream cones. The two were having a great time visiting Walt Disney World in Florida. However, these two people were not old men but eight-year-old boys with a rare genetic disorder called progeria. Progeria is a condition in which the person ages prematurely. It is characterized by dwarfism, baldness, pinched nose, delayed tooth formation, wrinkled skin, and early death. Only about one child in 8 million has the condition.

These children suffer from the very rare genetic disease progeria, which causes premature aging. Affected individuals rarely live past childhood.

On April 17, 2003, scientists announced they had found the gene responsible for progeria. The disorder is caused by a mutation in the gene *Lamin A*, found on chromosome 1.

MILD ALZHEIMER'S DISEASE

SIGNS OF MILD AD	WHAT'S NORMAL?
Difficulty learning and remembering new information. One of the most common signs of early dementia is forgetting recently learned information.	Investigators for the National Institute on Aging have studied normal aging. Although the number of brain neurons may decline somewhat, forgetting names or appointments occasionally is perfectly normal. Even healthy teenagers do this.
Difficulty managing finances, planning meals, taking medication on schedule. A person who has always been careful about balancing a checkbook suddenly overdraws the account many times. The person may make unusual purchases on a credit card. Forgetting to take medication or taking the wrong medication is common. Everyday things that take planning become difficult. The individual may begin to lose track of the steps involved in playing a game or making a telephone call.	Everyone has moments when they do not remember why they came into a room or what they planned to say, but this happens only occasionally.
Depression symptoms; someone with AD may have rapid mood swings that go from calm to tears to anger for no apparent reason.	At times, everyone feels sad, but typically a reason for the sadness is apparent.
Inability to do activities such as driving a car. The person may still remember how to put the keys in the car and drive, but he or she may get lost in his or her own neighborhood and not know how to get home.	Anyone can get lost in a strange city or unfamiliar place, but not in their own neighborhood. Ingrained activities can be performed without extra mental effort.

At this stage the person may begin to complain about his or her memory. If he or she is still working, he or she may not be doing his or her job correctly; when a problem is pointed out, he or she may deny that the problem happened.

Moderate Alzheimer's Disease

In moderate AD, the damage to the brain is worsening and has spread to cover a larger area of the brain. The disease now affects the brain areas that control language, reasoning, sensory processing, and thought. The symptoms become more and more pronounced, and behavioral changes become a real problem. Now the person may forget old facts, have difficulty performing tasks, become agitated easily, have deficits in intellect and reasoning, and show a lack of concern for appearance.

Forgetting old facts

A person with moderate AD may continually repeat stories and/or may ask the same questions over and over. One woman whose grandfather was afflicted with AD told how he would just sit all day and thumb through magazines without ever looking at the pages. To fill in gaps, the person may make up stories.

Difficulty performing tasks

At this stage the person has difficulty following notes and using the shower or toilet. Taking a bath can be a major obstacle. Some people may resist assistance, making a caregiver's job more difficult. At an AD support group, one man spoke about how he was trying to get his wife in the shower, and she pushed him in and shut the shower door.

Appearance of agitation

The person may argue more often, get irritated more easily, and become angry over unimportant, seemingly insignificant incidents.

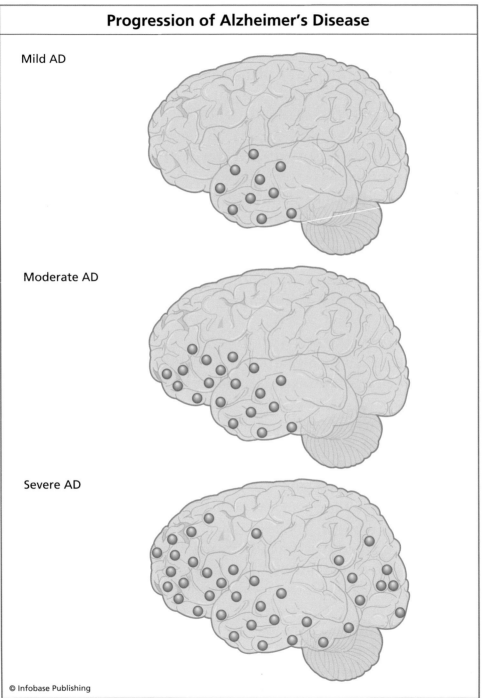

Progression of Alzheimer's Disease

Mild AD

Moderate AD

Severe AD

Restlessness and repetitive motions

Some people with AD get restless at the same time every afternoon. **Sundown syndrome** describes episodes of confusion, agitation, and disorientation that occur in the late afternoon into the evening. Scientists think that waning light at the end of the day triggers a chemical reaction in the brain that worsens AD symptoms. Sundown syndrome can be exhausting for the person with AD and his or her caregivers.

Paranoia, delusions, and hallucinations

Personalities may change dramatically. A person may become confused, suspicious, fearful, or dependent on a family member.

Lack of concern for appearance, hygiene, and sleep become more noticeable

Those persons with AD may dress inappropriately. For example, they may wear layers of clothes on a hot day, or little or nothing at all in the cold.

Moderate-stage Alzheimer's is very difficult for caregivers. The person with AD may become abusive or even violent toward the caregiver. They may even break the law. Unsafe driving, shoplifting, indecent exposure, and abuse to others are not uncommon.

Severe AD

In the advanced stage of AD, damage to the brain's nerve cells has become widespread. This is an even more difficult stage for family and caregivers. The person may have

(opposite page) **FIGURE 3.2** This progression shows the increasing spread of damage (*brown dots*) in different areas of the brain at the three stages of Alzheimer's disease.

difficulty walking and may suffer more easily from com-
plications of other diseases, such as pneumonia. Signs of
this stage include verbal outbursts, behavioral difficulties,

WHAT LAW ENFORCEMENT PERSONNEL NEED TO KNOW

The Alzheimer's Association trains law enforcement officers to deal with situations involving people with AD. The following includes some pertinent information.

People with AD may wander off:
Average distance of locating the individual alive is 0–5 miles.
They offer no cries for help.
They do not respond to shouts.
They may wander away to find a place where they have previously lived.
Individuals who leave in cars are generally found within the radius of one tank of gas; they may abandon the car when the gas runs out.
They may be afraid of law enforcement officers and may not recognize the uniform.

What Law Enforcement Needs to Do:
Search immediately.
Issue radio and media reports of the missing person.
Approach the person from the front and introduce yourself.
Let the person know you are there to help.

_____

Adapted from Alzheimer's Guide, Florida Chapters of the Alzheimer's Association, supported by the Florida Department of Law Enforcement.

failure to recognize family or faces, and difficulty with all essential activities of daily living. The person may become passive and sit in front of the TV for hours or may sleep more than usual, not wanting to do anything. As the disease progresses, the person may stay in bed for hours lying in the fetal position.

DIAGNOSING AND EVALUATING AD

Although a true diagnosis of Alzheimer's disease can only be made by examination of the brain at autopsy, a skilled physician can diagnose Alzheimer's with a high degree of accuracy. A person with possible AD behaviors should be encouraged to see a doctor, who will perform an examination and order tests. Several conditions, such as stroke, head injury, nutritional deficiencies, and certain kidney or lung diseases, can cause symptoms similar to AD. These conditions must be ruled out before a diagnosis of AD can be made.

Typically, the doctor will begin with a normal examination, like anyone might experience when going for a routine physical. The evaluation includes the patient's complete health history. The doctor will ask about the patient's physical and mental condition. If the person has had heart problems, hardening of the arteries, or small strokes, this is especially noted. There appears to be a connection between these conditions and AD. The physician then will check the person's neurological status and mental status, using any of several mental screening instruments, such as the Global Deterioration Scale (GDS), Brief Cognitive Rating Scale (BCRS), and the FAST scale.

The doctor may perform a variety of medical tests. Studies of the blood, urine, and spinal fluid may reveal infections that can be treated. An **electrocardiograph (EKG)** is used to check the heart, looking for anything abnormal. Chest

X-rays are also typically taken. A doctor may also use **electroencephalography (EEG)**, a procedure in which small electrodes are placed on the head to study brain waves. The doctor will also assess the patient's medications to determine whether certain medicines are causing the problem.

Other Powerful Tools

Some of the imaging technologies and other identification techniques used in diagnosing AD are also important tools in AD research. Noninvasive neuroimaging techniques yield pictures of the living brain, giving researchers a good idea of what is going on. Many diseases, including stroke, tumors, vascular disease, poisoning, nutritional deficiencies, infection, and depression, can mimic the symptoms of AD. Neuroimaging can help rule out dementia caused by one of the long list of diseases that are similar to AD. Some of these diseases can be treated. When all other conditions are ruled out, then it is diagnosed as "probable Alzheimer's."

The technologies most helpful in diagnosing AD are **magnetic resonance imaging (MRI)**, **computed tomography (CT)**, **positron emission tomography (PET)**, and **functional magnetic resonance imaging (fMRI).**

An MRI is probably most useful in measuring brain structures of people who may be in the earliest stages of AD. The MRI scan might also be used to find people who have had head injuries or mini-strokes, who might later be diagnosed with AD. Looking at the structure of the hippocampus could indicate those with mild cognitive impairment. The hippocampus is one of the first areas that AD affects. MRIs use a powerful magnet to create a two- or three-dimensional picture of anatomical structures.

An X-ray produces a two-dimensional image. X-ray techniques use a stationary machine that focuses beams of radiation on an area of the body—for example, a broken bone. CT scans add the third dimension. A CT scan uses an X-ray generating device that rotates around the body and uses a powerful computer to create cross-sectional images, like slices of the brain. The CT scan can pinpoint tumors or evidence of a stroke or brain shrinkage with a high degree of precision.

PET is a nuclear medical imaging technique, which produces a three-dimensional image or map of body processes. A short-lived radioactive tracer is injected into the body. The person is put into the imaging scanner. The radioactive positron decays and goes through a process that creates a burst of light, hitting a photo-sensitive tube. An expert can then read the data. PET is an important research tool used to map normal human brain functions.

PET is also used in preclinical studies for drug-testing on animals. Doctors at UCLA School of Medicine have developed a new technique using PET with a probe called FDDNP that creates three-dimensional pictures of the brain. Dr. Steve DeKosky and colleagues at the University of Pittsburgh created a compound called Pittsburgh Compound B, or PIB. PIB is injected into patients and produces areas of bright yellow, red, green, or blue when scanned, depending on the concentration of the plaque. Scans of people without AD appear black.

Functional MRI is a way of assessing the living brain in action, as the person performs a task during the scan. Scans show activity in certain areas where the blood supply is increased. The tool is controversial and not as useful in AD research except for memory processing studies.

After the evaluation, the physician can sometimes rule out stroke or other conditions. When tests for all other conditions are negative, a diagnosis of "probable AD" is made. There are many new tests that are being developed for screening, but these are still in the testing phase and may not be covered by insurance. Keep in mind that there is no one test that proves a person has Alzheimer's disese. Currently, only autopsy of the brain tissues can provide a definitive diagnosis of AD.

MEET THE
HUMAN GENOME

In the early nineteenth century, in an area of what is now the Czech Republic, a humble monk worked diligently in his garden. For nine years, Gregor Mendel studied various traits in peas plants and noted the patterns of inheritance for the traits. If he crossed purebred tall plants with purebred short plants, all of the offspring were tall. When he crossed those tall plants, he found that among the offspring, there were three tall plants to one short one. He performed the experiments over and over and found that same ratio each time. He then experimented with seven other traits, such as the shape of the seeds and the colors of the peas. The trait that appeared in the most abundance in these crosses, he called **dominant**; the other trait, he termed **recessive**.

When he presented his experiments in a paper in 1865, a few people were interested. However, most of his work was ignored until the beginning of the twentieth century, when the geneticist Thomas Hunt Morgan found these same principles applied to fruit flies. These principles came to be referred to as **Mendelian laws**, and interest in genetics, the scientific study of heredity, exploded over the course of the twentieth century.

In order to understand how Alzheimer's disease and genetics fit together, it is essential to look at the background of human genes. Many diseases of genetic origin can be traced to a change or mutation in only one gene. The genetics of AD is not so simple and involves many genes. To grasp how genes play a role in AD, this chapter includes a primer of the fundamentals of genetics, with an explanation of some of the important concepts—genes, DNA, proteins, chromosomes, transcription, and codons.

WHAT IS A GENE?

In 1663, Robert Hooke, a British scientist, peered through his crude microscope at a piece of cork and was interested in what he saw. Here was a cluster of structures that reminded him of monks' "cells," or sleeping quarters. The name "cell" stuck and was eventually applied to the approximately 100 trillion cells that are the basic building blocks of humans. All living plants and animals are made up of cells.

Over the years, scientists have discovered that all cells, with only a few exceptions, have some components in common: a nucleus, a cytoplasm, and a cell membrane. The central part of the cell, the nucleus, regulates all the cell's activities. In the nucleus are structures called **chromosomes**. The word "chromosome" comes from two Greek words: *chromo*, meaning "color," and *some*, meaning "body." In a cell that is dividing, the stained chromosomes appear as dark-colored bodies. In human cells, there are 22 pairs of chromosomes called **somatic chromosome**, also called autosomes, and one pair of **sex chromosomes**. The two sex chromosomes in females are X chromosomes; males have one X and one Y chromosome. Thus, humans have a total of 23 pairs of chromosomes.

Each chromosome contains a single long, coiled molecule of **deoxyribonucleic acid (DNA)**. DNA carries the blueprint of one's heredity. DNA structure is often described as a "twisted ladder." The rungs consist of pairs of nitrogen-containing bases and the pairing of the bases is highly specific. The rails, or sides, of the "ladder" are made of sugar-phosphate chains.

In 1953, James Watson and Francis Crick announced to the world that they had made a model of DNA. Working from X-rays of the molecule, they created a Tinker-toy-like complex of the twisted ladder with colored balls that made the base pairs.

For about 30 years after the structure of DNA was determined, the DNA of people, ants, and pine trees remained as unexplored as the deep recesses of space. All of this changed in the 1980s. With advances in technology that made it possible to determine the sequence of the bases in the DNA, DNA became the molecule to study, and the exploding growth of knowledge revealed some startling results. For example, scientists found that each chromosome has a long string of genes that codes for proteins, as well as a long stretch of DNA that does not appear to have any function. Scientists initially called this "junk DNA." Now they call it "noncoding DNA," and many believe that this part of DNA will be found to have regulatory and other functions.

DNA, like the hard drive of a computer, stores chunks of information. These chunks of information are the **genes**. Information in the gene, which is just a small part of DNA, is copied into a molecule called messenger **ribonucleic acid** (mRNA). RNA makes a template for protein synthesis. **RNA** then uses this information to direct the creation of the **proteins** that do the cell's work.

The process by which information from DNA is copied into RNA begins when the double-stranded DNA "unzips," forming two single strands. One of these strands serves as a "template," or model, for the synthesis of the RNA. The process by which the information in the single-stranded

DNA Structure

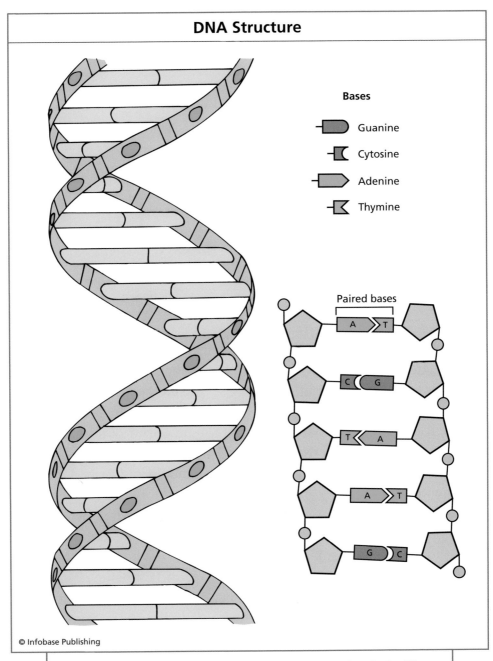

Bases

Guanine

Cytosine

Adenine

Thymine

Paired bases

A — T

C — G

T — A

A — T

G — C

FIGURE 4.1 The DNA molecule is a double helix that looks like a twisted ladder. The steps of the ladder are made up of small molecules called *bases*.

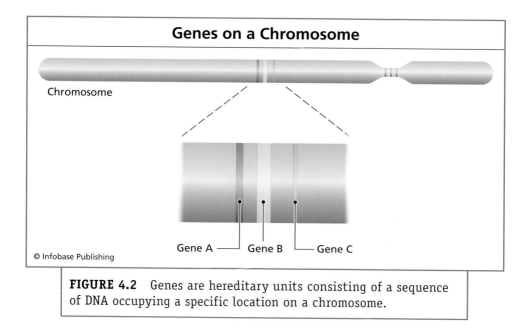

Genes on a Chromosome

Chromosome

Gene A —   — Gene B   — Gene C

© Infobase Publishing

FIGURE 4.2   Genes are hereditary units consisting of a sequence of DNA occupying a specific location on a chromosome.

DNA is copied into RNA is called **transcription.** The RNA created by transcription is called messenger RNA because it carries this information from the cell nucleus, where DNA is found, to the cytoplasm, where protein synthesis takes place. Remember that DNA holds the blueprint of heredity, but does not directly participate in doing the work. The work of making proteins, the building blocks of life, is done by RNA.

DNA is made up of subunits called **nucleotides**, which consist of a nitrogen-containing base, a phosphate molecule, and a sugar molecule. There are four different bases in DNA: adenine (A), guanine (G), thymine (T), and cytosine (C). In RNA, uracil (U) replaces thymine. In the double-stranded structure of a DNA molecule, the bases make up the "rungs"

(opposite page) **FIGURE 4.3**   During transcription, one DNA strand is used as a template to produce messenger RNA molecules.

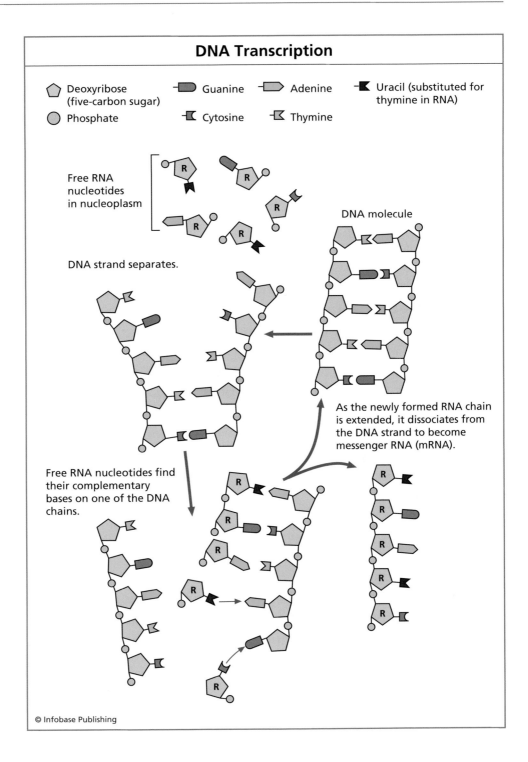

DNA Transcription

Deoxyribose (five-carbon sugar)

Phosphate

Guanine

Adenine

Uracil (substituted for thymine in RNA)

Cytosine

Thymine

Free RNA nucleotides in nucleoplasm

DNA molecule

DNA strand separates.

As the newly formed RNA chain is extended, it dissociates from the DNA strand to become messenger RNA (mRNA).

Free RNA nucleotides find their complementary bases on one of the DNA chains.

of the ladder described above. They pair together very specifically, adenine (A) with thymine (T) and cytosine (C) with guanine (G). In RNA, adenine (A) pairs with uracil (U). Sequences of millions of these base pairs can make up a single gene. The sugar in DNA is deoxyribose. Deoxyribose is a 5-carbon sugar formed by enzymes in living cells.

In a strand of DNA, a sequence of three adjacent nucleotides is a **codon.** Each codon designates the creation of a particular **amino acid.** An amino acid is an organic compound containing an amino (NH_2) group and an organic acid (COOH). They link together by peptide bonds to form protein molecules.

What, then, is a gene? A gene is a sequence of nucleotides within the DNA that specifies the order in which amino acids should be linked to form a protein. The control of protein synthesis allows the gene to determine the characteristics of not only the cell, but ultimately whether the person will have traits such as blue eyes or brown skin, or a genetic disease, such as Alzheimer's disease. Most genes are about 1,000 to 4,000 nucleotides long. The entire complement of a person's DNA is called the **genome.**

THE HUMAN GENOME PROJECT

In 1987, the Department of Energy recommended a project to map and identify all the base pairs of the human genome. The target date was 2005. James Watson, codiscoverer of DNA's structure in 1953, kicked off the **Human Genome Project** as director in 1990. Watson resigned in 1992 and Francis Collins, a researcher from the University of Michigan, took over.

The director of the project sent the actual sequencing to centers in the United States, Japan, England, and China. Many teams worked on different parts of the chromosomes.

Producing maps of the genome involves three important processes:

- ◆ Cutting DNA molecules using **restriction enzymes**, enzymes that cut DNA in certain places.
- ◆ *Cloning*, or copying the fragments.
- ◆ Finding overlapping fragments to analyze.

Another player soon entered the game. J. Craig Venter, a researcher at the National Institutes of Health (NIH), announced he had developed a new machine called a DNA sequencer that could identify thousands of genes at a time. The other investigators were studying only one gene at a time. This process let him bypass the noncoding DNA that

KARY MULLIS AND COPIES OF DNA

Kary Mullis, a scientist at Cetus Corporation, was riding along the hills of Northern California one moonlit night. As his mind wandered to his work, he thought about how amazing the process of DNA replication was. Suddenly, the idea popped into his head: Why can this not be done with a machine?

The idea was so straightforward that he had a hard time convincing his company that it could work. He built a machine that takes a piece of DNA through cycles, with the end product being many copies of the piece of DNA. The procedure is called **polymerase chain reaction (PCR)**. The machine takes a piece of DNA and makes it into a piece that is detectable. For example, a small bit of tissue left at a crime scene can be amplified to show the killer was there.

PCR has changed the whole field of genetics. For his vision, Mullis won the Nobel Prize in Chemistry in 1993.

makes up 95% of the genome. Venter formed a private company called Celera that promised to sequence the genome years before 2005.

In June 2000, President Bill Clinton stood beside Collins and Venter and announced that a rough draft of the genome had been completed well ahead of the target date. What did this mean? They had identified all of the base pairs on the various chromosomes. Initially, it was thought that there were 50,000 to 100,000 genes made from 3 billion base pairs. Their research revealed that the number of human genes was actually nearer 25,000. The real work, however, still lay ahead. They had to determine exactly which genes programmed for which proteins and how these proteins worked.

A PRIMER ON PROTEINS

Understanding proteins is essential to understanding Alzheimer's disease. What are proteins and how are they made? That process by which mRNA directs the construction of protein molecules is called **translation**.

There are 20 different amino acids used to build proteins. These amino acids can be assembled in a vast number of ways. The arrangement, or sequence, of amino acids determines the primary structure of the protein. The chain of amino acids may twist, coil, and fold back on itself, making it a very complex molecule.

Understanding how proteins are synthesized and how they work is essential in understanding the complex molecules that are involved in AD research. In a cell, multitudes of proteins perform many functions. The biggest single class of proteins is **enzymes**, chemicals that speed up all the chemical reactions in a living organism. One cell may contain as many as 3,000 enzymes.

The Arrangement of Amino Acids in Proteins

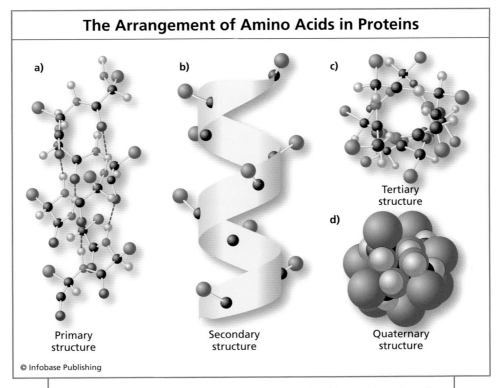

a)

b)

c)

Tertiary
structure

d)

Primary
structure

Secondary
structure

Quaternary
structure

© Infobase Publishing

FIGURE 4.4 Amino acids link together to build proteins. Protein structure can be categorized in four ways: primary, which shows the order of the different amino acids in the protein; secondary, in which the amino acid chain takes a specific geometric shape, such as a helix; tertiary, in which the structure of the protein folds into itself; and quaternary, which illustrates how proteins connect to each other.

It is amazing that a code using sequences of only three bases, known as triplets, in a DNA molecule can provide the information needed to specify the sequence of the 20 different amino acids in thousands of proteins. These amazing three-letter codes work this way. Each triplet, or codon, specifies one particular amino acid. For example, AAA, which is a sequence of three adenine bases, codes for the amino acid lysine, and CCC, a sequence of three cytosine bases, codes for the amino acid proline. Therefore, where there is an AAA sequence in mRNA, there will be lysine in the forming chain of amino acids that will eventually make a protein. Where there is a CCC sequence in the mRNA, there will be a proline in the forming amino acid chain.

In summary, DNA is not directly involved in protein synthesis; it simply provides the initial instructions. DNA unzips and one strand is used as a template to make messenger RNA. mRNA is a key intermediary in translating the DNA's genetic code into amino acids that make up proteins. The RNA, with its copy of the genetic code, passes out of the nucleus and into the cell cytoplasm. Codons along the messenger RNA control the sequence of amino acids in a forming protein.

If written out, the human genome's 3 billion letters would require nearly 1,000 volumes, each as long as a Harry Potter novel. How can anyone possibly make sense out of all these letters to find genes that cause disease? How dedicated scientists have identified these genes is a fascinating story that is still unraveling.

5

FINDING FAULTY GENES

In the late 1980s and early 1990s, and again in a recent movie, the Teenage Mutant Ninja Turtles became heroes to children everywhere. In this fictional saga, the human-like turtles Leonardo, Donatello, Raphael, and Michelangelo fight their way to victory over the evil ninja named Shredder. The turtles had mutated, or changed, in the sewers of New York into unique creatures that could do things normal turtles could not. Few moviegoers or video game players realized that the turtles had introduced young children to the concept of mutations.

CHANGES IN GENES AND GENETIC DISEASES

The mutant turtles were a fantasy, but mutations are real. A **mutation** is any permanent change in the structure of DNA. Chapter 4 discussed how proteins are made during the process of translation. Think of the process of translation like a group of people on an assembly line making a large number of peanut butter and jelly sandwiches. Each person has a job: One person opens the bread, another spreads the peanut butter, another spreads the jelly, and another puts the slices of bread together. The assembly line moves like clockwork. Then the jelly spreader drops his knife and

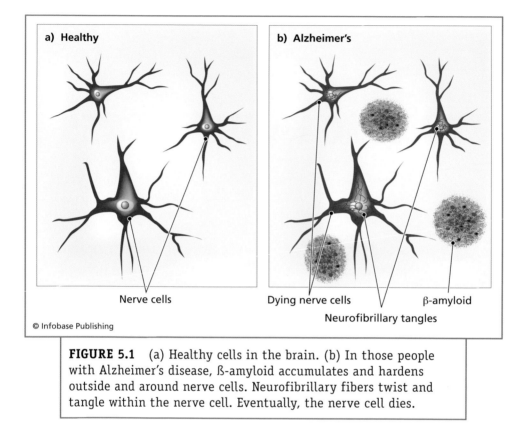

a) Healthy

b) Alzheimer's

Nerve cells

Dying nerve cells

β-amyloid

Neurofibrillary tangles

© Infobase Publishing

FIGURE 5.1   (a) Healthy cells in the brain. (b) In those people with Alzheimer's disease, ß-amyloid accumulates and hardens outside and around nerve cells. Neurofibrillary fibers twist and tangle within the nerve cell. Eventually, the nerve cell dies.

has to go under the table to get it; he takes time to wash the knife. The assembly line keeps moving, but now no jelly is on the sandwiches; they are only peanut butter sandwiches. This simple illustration shows how just one small slip can change the outcome of a product. Even a small change in the structure of DNA can affect the structure and function of the protein specified by the DNA.

THE ROLE OF FAULTY PROTEINS

Researchers have become increasingly aware of the role that mutations play in the development of a disease such as AD. Various factors outside the body, such as food, polluted air or water, ultraviolet radiation, and chemicals, are known to cause mutations in genes; they are *mutagens*. A gene with a mutation can produce a faulty protein. In turn, these faulty proteins can lead to diseases such as Alzheimer's disease.

As noted previously, a definitive diagnosis of Alzheimer's disease is made only by examination of the brain at autopsy. Here are some of the abnormalities that are seen in the brain of a person with AD:

♦ Alzheimer's patients will show extensive deposits, or plaques, of β-amyloid, a sticky protein that appears like tangled threads. (The β stands for *beta*, and is the second letter of the Greek alphabet.) β-amyloid is snipped from a larger protein called amyloid precursor protein, or APP. Surrounding the plaques are bits of dying nerve cells. These cells are astrocytes and microglial cells, which are kinds of glial cells. Glial cells support, nourish, and protect the neurons of the brain and spinal cord. The word *microglial* comes from two Greek words, *micro* meaning "small," and *glia* meaning "glue."

♦ Twisted nerve cell fibers, known as neurofibrillary tangles (NFTs). NFTs are formed in the nerve cell when damaged tau proteins, which normally stabilize the nerve cell, become tangled with normal tau inside the cell body.

Scientists have studied the chemical structure of these proteins. Finding the genes that are responsible for making the proteins has been a task that rivals any detective story.

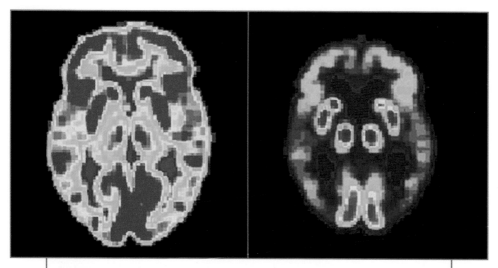

FIGURE 5.2 Positron emission tomography (PET) scans show the metabolic activity in a normal brain (a) compared to the decline in metabolic activity shown in a brain with Alzheimer's disease (b).

RUDOLPH TANZI: DECODER OF DARKNESS

Rudolph Tanzi traveled along a Boston street on a cloudy September day in 1980. As a college graduate with degrees in both microbiology and history, he had heard of an opening in the laboratory of James Gusella at Harvard University. Tanzi got the job to help him pay off the expenses of graduate school. Gusella was in the midst of a project linking Huntington's disease, a serious nerve disease, with specific genes.

While working as a graduate student in the lab, Tanzi attended a lecture by Dennis Selkoe, an up-and-coming Alzheimer's disease researcher. Selkoe spoke about how amyloid collected in the brain's blood vessels and clung to the walls. Selkoe then presented a slide that became the defining moment in Tanzi's life. It was a slide of Alexander the Great cutting the Gordian knot. In Greek mythology, the Gordian knot was an intricate knot that no one could undo until Alexander tried a new way that no one had thought of before: He cut the knot with his sword. Selkoe said that amyloid was like the knot; it would take someone with dedication and out-of-the-box thinking to solve the puzzle. Because the puzzle could not be easily "untied," no one was meeting that challenge.

This speech challenged Tanzi, and the renegade protein β-amyloid became his passion. Remembering Gusella's research on the gene that caused Huntington's disease, he set out to locate the gene that was responsible for Alzheimer's disease. His research took him to chromosome 21. By the end of 1987, he and his colleagues had located a gene called *APP* (amyloid precursor protein). He finished his thesis on Patriot's Day of 1990, just in time to run the Boston Marathon. Currently, Tanzi is a well-known molecular geneticist and professor of neurology at Harvard Medical School. In his autobiography, Tanzi detailed his search for the genetic causes of Alzheimer's. The book is titled *Decoding Darkness*.

FINDING FAULTY GENES

How do scientists such as Tanzi go about finding a particular faulty gene? While it appears to be a daunting task, there are several strategies that geneticists use. To locate a suspected gene, geneticists create maps that describe the location of a particular gene on a chromosome. One type of map is made by applying gene sequencing. As we have seen, genes are sequences of DNA. Sequencing hunts for those genes and finds their places on chromosomes. The Human Genome Project sequenced the nucleotide letters on all of the human chromosomes. Sequencing is done with powerful computers. After a possible sequence is found, it is stored in a database. Computers then scan thousands of entries comparing the same gene in different species. Three techniques are used to develop other information about AD: transgenic animals, twin studies, and quantitative trait loci (QTL).

Transgenic Animals

Researchers have been able to create animals that have symptoms of Alzheimer's. The animals—typically mice— have been created using genes transferred from other animals, even humans. The term *transgenic* comes from two Latin words: *trans*, meaning "across," and *gen*, meaning "gene." Thus, by transferring genes from one animal to another, scientists have created an animal that has symptoms similar to those of AD.

Other mice used in experiments are called "knockout" mice because scientists have knocked out, or inactivated, certain genes. The loss of the genes causes changes in the mice and gives researchers an idea of the function of the normal genes.

By late 1991, three successful Alzheimer mouse models were developed. The mice exhibited signs of dementia. They withdrew, forgot how to run mazes, and even forgot how to find food. When scientists performed autopsies, they found the brains of the animals showed the tell-tale plaques and tangles of AD. Having animal models was a real breakthrough, not only for scientists investigating the basic biology of AD, but also for researchers looking for drugs to dissolve the plaques. In order for the U.S. Food and Drug Administration (FDA) to approve a drug, the pharmaceutical company must test the drug on animals.

Twin Studies

The genome for any two human beings, regardless of ethnic or racial identity, is about 99.9% identical. Identical twins, however, have identical DNA. They developed from a single fertilized egg that split to form two separate individuals. Twins are useful for studying inherited traits because they have the same traits, and often develop the same diseases and disorders due to their identical genetic code. Studies of identical twins who were raised in different households have helped researchers understand the roles of genetics and environmental influences in the development of AD.

A large study of twins completed in 2006 found a strong genetic basis for AD. Margaret Gatz, a researcher at the University of Southern California, led a team that studied 12,000 identical and fraternal twins who were age 65 and older. The researchers found 392 pairs with one or both members showing symptoms of AD. Identical twin pairs in which both twins developed AD suggested a genetic influence for AD development. The existence of identical twin pairs in which one member developed AD but the other did not suggested that environmental influences such as a person's diet, or episodes such as a stroke or a fall, can make a difference in whether or not a person develops AD. The data revealed that genetic influence accounted for 79% of AD **risk**. Risk means that the factors are strong for developing the disease. The risk for men was the same as the risk for women. The 21% who did not have symptoms of the disease, however, also provided important information. The 21% showed that major environmental influences are at work. Lifestyle events such as stroke, falls, or diet can make a difference in AD.

Quantitative Trait Loci (QTL)

The term **quantitative trait loci** (QTL) refers to stretches of DNA that are closely linked to the genes that underlie the trait in question. Scientists can trace the trait through many different generations and then look through the genome of relatives to find a gene that might match. The term *locus* ("loci" being the plural of locus) refers to a particular place on a chromosome where the gene is located.

Scientists, using QTL, have traced AD through several generations of mice. Using mouse models to trace the generations has been helpful because mice produce several generations in a year. Tracing AD in humans is a more difficult

THE HUNT FOR THE HUNTINGTON'S GENE

Nancy Wexler, a psychologist, watched her mother slowly deteriorate from Huntington's disease, a disease that destroys the nervous system. People do not begin to show the symptoms of this disease until their thirties. She knew that the disease ran in families.

On a program on the Discovery channel, she saw villagers with the same struggling walk as her mother in a village on Lake Maracaibo in Venezuela. She made her way to Venezuela and convinced the villagers to give blood samples. Wexler sent the blood samples to James Gusella at Harvard University for analysis. Wexler made a huge genetic map of the people with the disease and then Gusella used genetic sequencing to match the DNA from blood samples with the map, looking for a genetic marker that linked the cases of Huntingon's. This procedure led them to the gene that causes Huntington's disease.

process. At the beginning of the twentieth century, world-wide life expectancy was only about 40 years, so there were fewer recorded cases of AD. However, as life expectancy increased, a small number of large families, whose members developed AD at around age 50, did keep records. This type of AD became known as familial Alzheimer's disease (FAD). Scientists traveled to distant parts of the world to draw genetic maps. From their maps, they could determine that FAD is a dominant disorder. That meant that if either the mother or father had the condition, their children would have a fifty-fifty chance of inheriting it.

Another important clue to the genetics of AD came when scientists noted that people with Down syndrome almost always developed dementia in their forties. People with Down syndrome have an extra chromosome 21. When autopsies of people with Down syndrome showed plaques and tangles, researchers began to think there was a connection between chromosome 21 and AD. In 1987, Peter St. George-Hyslop, along with Rudolph Tanzi, located the amyloid precursor gene on chromosome 21. This gene codes for the protein amyloid.

The three methods—transgenic animals, twin studies, and QTL—have given geneticists a lot of information about AD. These methods form the basis of the genetic approach to learning about disease.

Finding faulty genes is a challenge. Researchers have worked to find not only the causes but the mechanics behind them. There are three areas of research that relate to AD: basic, applied, and clinical.

◆ Scientists conduct basic research when they look for what causes a condition. This research is mostly done on animals.

◆ Applied research occurs when the scientists, building on basic information, begin to apply what they know to the disease. At this stage, they may test drugs or other treatments on animals.

◆ Clinical research is done on humans. It starts with only a few people to test for the safety of a drug. Then more and more people are used.

Research on AD is progressing at all three levels. When the gene and the mechanisms behind it are found, then a possible cure may not be far behind.

THE ANSWER
IS IN THE GENES

In Greek mythology, Eos, the goddess of the dawn, fell in love with Tithonus, a mortal. She was so smitten that she begged Zeus to make her mortal lover live forever. Everything was great for a while, until Tithonus began to age. He lost his mind and could not remember anything. Eos had neglected to ask Zeus to grant eternal youth to Tithonus. The term "Tithonus effect" is applied to the situation in which people live a long time but are in very poor health and have a poor quality of life.

The Tithonus effect may illustrate many lives in the twenty-first century. Scientific advances have increased life expectancy. With aging and longer life, however, come mental and physical problems that may be overwhelming. One of the most prevalent predictors of risk for AD is age. AD is not an inevitable part of aging, but living longer does increase risk. The main risk factors for AD include:

◆ Age: Prevalence doubles with every decade after 60. Rudolph Tanzi presented the following figures in a speech titled "Molecular Genetics of Alzheimer's Disease":
  ◇ Prevalence in Americans under 60 = 5%
  ◇ Prevalence in Americans over 75 = 10%

◇   Prevalence in Americans over 85 = 20%–50%, with an average of 40%

◆   Family history: Risk is higher for relatives of affected individuals, and even higher for individuals whose relatives had early-onset AD (younger than 60).

IS AD TYPE 3 DIABETES?

Diabetes is a disease in which either the body does not produce enough insulin or the body's cells cannot use insulin normally to remove glucose from the blood. In Type 1 diabetes, which was once called juvenile diabetes, the body produces little or no insulin. In Type 2 diabetes, the cells of the body become insensitive to insulin and cannot use it properly. Diabetes is a serious disease that can be connected with blindness, heart disease, stroke, kidney failure, and amputations. Some researchers include diabetes as a major risk factor for AD.

Canadian researchers have found β-amyloid, the same sticky plaque that clogs the brains of AD patients, in the pancreases of people with Type 2 diabetes. Some investigators ponder whether diabetes and AD are different forms of the same disease. Several studies have made the connection. A nine-year Canadian study of 1,175 individuals age 75 and older found borderline diabetes was associated with a 70% risk of developing AD.

Jack Diamond, scientific director of the Alzheimer's Association of Canada, said that some researchers are speculating that AD may actually be Type 3 diabetes. Already, thousands of people with AD in the United States are being given drugs such as Avandia and Actos, which treat diabetes. If the connection is made, drugs that have already been approved, along with diet and exercise, may prove useful in treating and preventing AD.

◆ Gender: AD is more common in women. Tanzi questioned possible hormone connections.
◆ Life exposure factors:
  ◇ Head trauma
  ◇ High cholesterol
  ◇ Type 2 diabetes
  ◇ Lack of mental stimulation

The genetic approach to disease has been the subject of a great deal of research. Tanzi outlined how scientists use the genetic approach to disease:

1. Identify all the gene variations associated with the disease.
2. Demonstrate the links between these gene variations and the pathology of the disease.
3. Establish genetic profiles to identify subjects at high risk for early prediction of the disease.
4. Try to develop novel strategies to intervene with the disease.

This chapter focuses on what scientists have discovered about the genetic basis of AD. In particular, the genes that are believed to be involved in AD are discussed.

CHROMOSOMES ASSOCIATED WITH AD
Chromosome 21 and FAD

Familial Alzheimer's disease (FAD) is a rare form of the disease that affects less than 10% of persons with AD. This type of disease progresses faster than the common late-onset forms.

Using genetic sequencing, the researchers found an abnormal gene for FAD on chromosome 21. That gene, which expresses the protein called amyloid precursor protein, differed from the normal gene by only one base pair. In 1991, the DNA sequence established that the mutant gene on chromosome 21 was associated with FAD.

Three connections with chromosome 21 were present:

◆ A genetic defect causes the formation of a defective amyloid protein.
◆ The defective amyloid protein is deposited in certain places in the cerebral cortex.
◆ The deposit destroys neurons and produces the clinical symptoms of AD.

Researchers began to think they had found a strong association between AD and a gene on chromosome 21. However, the connection was not so simple to confirm. Only about 2% to 3% of FAD cases were associated with this gene. Other researchers began to find families with AD that did not have the amyloid precursor protein gene. About a year after the gene was found on chromosome 21, another gene emerged as a stronger candidate.

Chromosome 14

Chromosome 14 became a candidate for AD when statistics showed a common marker for the defective amyloid protein on chromosome 14. This time the investigators named the gene *presenilin 1* (*PS-1*). Researchers are looking at how presenilins work.

Chromosome 1

Researchers also found a group of Germans who lived in the Volga Valley of the former Soviet Union and had a very high occurrence of AD. The studies showed no link between the disease in these people and chromosomes 21 and 14. Then studies revealed a gene on a particular region of chromosome 1. This gene was called *presenilin 2 (PS-2)*. Only a small fraction of early-onset FAD is caused by mutations in the *presenilin 2* gene.

The mutations in three genes—*APP, presenilin 1,* and *presenilin 2*—account for about 50% of early-onset FAD. If individuals have inherited these genes, they are definitely at risk for developing the disease. Other genes associated with FAD have yet to be identified.

Chromosome 19

The genetics of late-onset AD is much more complicated than that of FAD. There are some gene forms that occur more often in people with AD than in the population in general. In 1992, researchers at Duke University in North Carolina found an increased risk for late-onset AD with the inheritance of one or two copies of a gene called ***apolipoprotein epsilon***, or ***APOE***, which is located on chromosome 19.

The protein made by this gene is called APOE. It sits on the surface of cholesterol molecules; cholesterol is a form of fat that is both manufactured by the body and consumed by eating animal fat. APOE helps carry the cholesterol in the blood throughout the body. APOE is found in glial cells (the cells that hold neurons together) and nerve cells of healthy brains. It is also found in the plaques and neurofibrillary tangles in AD brains.

The different forms of a gene are called **alleles.** For every gene, a person inherits one allele from each parent. Every person has two *APOE* genes, one inherited from each parent. *APOE* has three different alleles: *APOE-epsilon2, APOE-epsilon3,* and *APOE-epsilon4*. The Greek symbol for epsilon is ε. APOE-ε3 is the normal form of the protein; APOE-ε2 and APOE-ε4 are disease-causing forms. The *APOE* gene has 3,597 base pairs. The alleles differ from one another by only a single base-pair; the substitutions of incorrect bases occur at positions 112 and 158.

The *APOE-ε4* gene is associated with atherosclerosis, or hardening of the arteries, and AD. In fact, *APOE-ε4* has been shown to cause an increased susceptibility to AD. Forty to sixty percent of the people with AD have at least one copy of *APOE-ε4*. People who inherit one copy of the *APOE-ε4* allele have an increased chance of developing the disease; those who inherit two copies of the allele are at even greater risk. Not all people with AD, however, have the *APOE-ε4* allele, and not all people who have the *APOE-ε4* allele will develop the disease.

GENES AND AD

Scientists continue to search for new genes that might be involved in AD. A number of studies have reported associations between specific forms of known genes and late-onset AD. Like *APOE ε-4*, the genes only increase the risk; they are not the cause.

Researchers at Duke University screened the entire genome in people from a group of families in which more than one member had late-onset AD. Using statistical analysis, researchers found four regions that might contain genes that put these families at higher risk for AD. The strongest pattern was on chromosome 12.

Tau is a protein that is correlated with the death of neurons. The genes that regulate it are largely unknown. Researchers from the University of Texas Medical School found a gene called *Dab1* that possibly interacts with *APOE*. QTL of mice deficient in *Dab1* showed that two regions contained genes that are defective in early onset AD.

Aging is generally considered a risk factor for AD. A study presented in 2006 marked the first time scientists found a

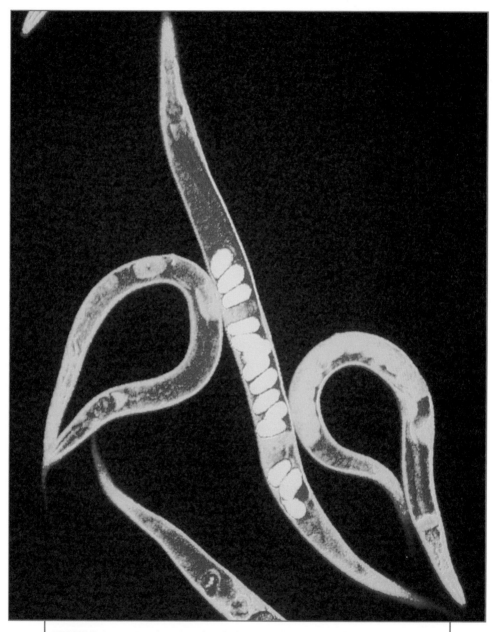

FIGURE 6.1   A micrograph of the roundworm *C. elegans,* an animal model used in testing because it has several of the same genes as humans. It takes only three days for the worm to reach maturity. The round structures inside the worm are eggs.

genetic link between aging and AD. This study proposes that AD may be a failure of the brain's ability to clean house as it gets older. The major cause of AD is the accumulation of the poisonous β-amyloid plaques both in the brain and outside brain cells. Andrew Dillin of the Salk Institute and Jeffrey Kelly of the Scripps Research Institute have located two genes that are responsible for preventing these proteins from accumulating. The two genes, *HSF-1* and *DAF-16*, are both less active with age; both are connected with early-onset Alzheimer's. *HSF-1* destroys toxic protein within the cell. *DAF-16* converts the toxic proteins into harmless lumps.

The discovery of the two genes is the first genetic and molecular link between aging and AD. The genes may also be a clue for possibly preventing AD. Kelly has developed technology that can detect the formation of toxic proteins at sensitivities 1,000 times greater than current techniques. The two scientists made their discoveries while studying *Caenorhabditis elegans,* a roundworm used widely as an animal model because it has several of the same genes as humans. The scientists are now studying the effects of several drugs on *C. elegans* that might boost *HSF-1*. Finding such a drug could possibly lead to the prevention of AD in humans.

In January 2007, scientists from 14 institutions announced that a new gene known as *Sorletin-related receptor 1,* or *SORL1,* may be a factor in the development of late-onset Alzheimer's disease. The faulty version of *SORL1* may contribute to the formation of amyloid plaques. As discussed previously, scientists have recognized three genes—*APP*, *PS-1*, and *PS-2*—that increase risk for early-onset AD. This discovery, however, was a completely new genetic clue about the late-onset forms. Knowing that *APP* is processed into the β-protein fragments that make plaques, researchers began looking for genetic influences amid a group of proteins that

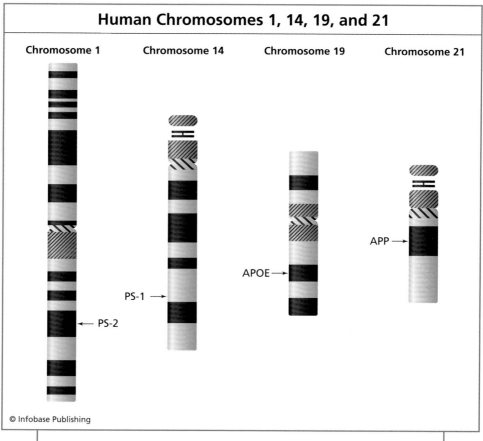

Human Chromosomes 1, 14, 19, and 21

Chromosome 1   Chromosome 14   Chromosome 19   Chromosome 21

APP →

APOE →

PS-1 →

← PS-2

© Infobase Publishing

FIGURE 6.2 Representations of chromosomes 1, 14, 19, 21, showing locations of genes for *presenilin 2* (*PS-2*), *presenilin 1* (*PS-1*), *apolipoprotein epsilon* (*APOE*), and *amyloid beta precursor protein* (*APP*).

carry *APP* within cells. They combed two large data sets of information and found the same association between *SORL1* in families with AD. Researchers note that much research must be done before any conclusions can be drawn.

The wealth of information about the possible genes involved in AD is accumulating so fast that it is difficult to follow and interpret it. Lars Bertram and others at the

Massachusetts Institute of Technology have created a database that catalogs all genetic association studies in the field of AD. They have found more than a dozen potential AD susceptibility genes. This database is a potential model for tracking the most viable gene candidates for AD.

7

IN SEARCH OF HELP

In the scientific method, the researcher keeps all the variables constant except the one that he or she is investigating. For example, a study of the effect of the amount of water on plants would require all test plants to have identical conditions of soil, sunlight, fertilizer, and so on. The only condition that would vary would be the amount of water the test plants received.

Scientists try to keep all variables constant except the one being tested when studying how a drug affects a disease or how people react to certain conditions. They may try to control variables by recruiting subjects with similar backgrounds. It is very difficult to do controlled studies of humans because they have so many different characteristics and lifestyles.

Studying Alzheimer's is like putting pieces of a puzzle together. The subjects are perplexing, and the research is complex.

Who would make ideal subjects for a study of Alzheimer's disease? An important criterion would be subjects who have shared and controlled lifestyles. Dr. David Snowdon, a professor at the University of Kentucky, found an ideal group of people for such a study. In 2004, he released a study of

678 nuns who were members of the School Sisters of Notre Dame. The sisters ranged in age from 75 to 106 and were very much alike in their diet and lifestyle habits. Nearly every nun had kept an autobiography or journal written over the course of her life. His research question: Why did some of the sisters age successfully past 100, while others became totally disconnected from the world around them as they aged?

Snowdon was given access to the nuns' files and autobiographies, which the convent carefully kept. The nuns agreed to donate their brains for study. The results of Snowdon's study are as follows:

- Stroke can trigger the symptoms of dementia in a person at risk for AD (collected from the brain study).
- Deficiency of folic acid, a B vitamin, tends to accelerate the brain-damaging effect of AD.
- Low education is a risk factor.
- Early brain development is important; those nuns who had low verbal skills in early life tended to develop AD 60 years after entering the convent as young women.
- On autopsy, 95% of the nuns had developed some of the plaques and tangles of AD, but only some showed the symptoms of AD.

Snowdon is using his research to develop a tremendous genetic library for scientists to access. He is only one of the many dedicated scientists studying AD.

This chapter is divided into two major sections. The first part presents information on research into finding methods to alleviate the symptoms and eventually find a cure for AD. The second part considers the needs of a person with AD and the responsibilities and challenges facing a caregiver.

DRUG DEVELOPMENT: SEARCH FOR A CURE

When the families of AD patients read about a new drug for AD, they often rush to ask their doctors about it. To such inquiries, the answer always is: No cure for AD exists yet. The U.S. Food and Drug Administration, however, lists AD drug testing at a high priority. More than 75 drugs are being studied, most of these for alleviating symptoms.

To understand medical research, one must know how drugs are developed. It is a difficult and time-consuming process. Pharmaceutical companies typically invest millions of dollars and many years to bring a new product to the market. It may take as long as 15 to 20 years from the start of development to get a drug approved for public use. Many drugs make it to the last phase of clinical trials (Phase III) and are then rejected.

TREATING AD WITH DRUGS

Understanding the types of drugs used to treat the symptoms of AD can be quite confusing. Although no cure exists, some drugs may help the person think, perceive, judge, and recognize their loved ones—at least for a little while. As the disease progresses, however, even these drugs do not work. Research is ongoing to test the effectiveness of AD drugs. It is important for a patient to consult a geriatrician for just the right medication.

As of 2007, the FDA had approved five medications for AD. Four of the approved drugs are part of a class that blocks the breakdown of a chemical messenger in the brain. The messengers, called neurotransmitters, carry impulses across

PROTOCOLS FOR CLINICAL TRIALS

RESEARCH STAGE	WHAT HAPPENS DURING THIS STAGE
Preclinical	This is the stage of basic research. Trials are conducted on mice, guinea pigs, monkeys, or other animals. This stage involves a lot of trial and error.
Phase I	If the preclinical research results in a good candidate for a drug, the company will apply to various government agencies for a new drug application. Contacting the FDA is the first step. If money is to be received from the National Institutes of Health (NIH), the company must have NIH approval. If the drug is to be genetically engineered, the company must apply to the Recombinant DNA Advisory Committee, which supervises cloning and gene therapy. Phase I trials are small and usually involve 2 to 20 people. These tests are primarily meant to test the safety of the drug.
Phase II	If Phase I is successful, researchers move to Phase II, which continues to study safety but also how well the drug works, or efficacy. Phase II trials generally involve 100 to 300 people.
Phase III	If Phase II shows the drug to be safe and effective, investigators recruit thousands of patients at a variety of centers. This phase is very expensive and time-consuming. Collecting the data is a massive job. Only after the trials are complete and generally successful does the FDA approve the drug and put it on the market.
Phase IV	After approval and marketing, the drug is monitored for long-term effects. The follow-ups may last from 10 to 20 years. The FDA may pull a drug from the market if a problem is uncovered. Celebrex was a popular arthritis drug that was pulled from the market because of a number of heart-related deaths connected to its use.

the gaps between one nerve cell and the next. They allow messages to travel from one part of the brain to another, and from one part of the body to another. Impulses from neighboring neurons arrive at the dendrites of a neuron. They travel to the cell body and then to the axon and across the gap, or **synapse**, between nerve cells, arriving at the dendrites of the next nerve cell.

One of the many different neurotransmitters in the body is a chemical called acetylcholine, which is important in memory and thought. As AD progresses, less and less acetylcholine circulates in the nervous system. One class of drugs stops the loss of acetylcholine temporarily. The enzyme that breaks down acetylcholine is called cholinesterase. Therefore, the class of drugs is named cholinesterase inhibitors. Four of the approved AD treatment drugs are cholinesterase inhibitors. These medicines inhibit the inactivation of acetylcholine by cholinesterase, so that concentrations of acetylcholine in the brain rise. The drug Cognex (tacrine) was the first to be approved, in 1993. It is rarely used now because it can cause severe liver damage. Today, the leading product for treatment is Aricept (donepezil), approved in 1996. Two others are Reminyl (galantamine hydrobromide) and Exelon (rivastigmine tartrate). The drugs are most effective if begun in the early stages and for mild to moderate AD. In October 2006, the FDA approved Aricept for the treatment of severe AD. In July 2007, the Exelon patch, the first skin patch for the treatment of mild to moderate Alzheimer's disease, was approved for use.

The newest AD drug, which reached the market in 2003, was memantine, marketed as Namenda. Namenda works in a different way. It keeps the brain cells from getting too much of another neurotransmitter called glutamate. Excess levels of glutamate contribute to death of brain cells in people with AD. Namenda has shown to be effective in people with more advanced AD.

Although none of these approved drugs target the under-lying cause of the disease, they can help some people improve quality of day-to-day life. As will be discussed in Chapter 8, there are some new medications and new ways of treating AD on the horizon.

Researchers suspect that no single "magic bullet" to cure the symptoms of AD exists. Instead, the treatment may be a combination or battery of drugs, each attacking the disease on a different level.

PREVENTION OF AD

Several current studies are focusing on prevention of AD. For most young people, a condition such as AD that may happen in later life seems unreal and far away. Keep in mind, however, that AD is correlated to events that happen earlier in one's life. One of the questions that people with early stages of AD are asked is, "Have you ever had a severe blow to the head?" Wearing a seat belt and a bike or ski helmet decrease the chances of developing AD by protecting the brain from such events.

Unhealthy lifestyle choices, such as lack of exercise and poor diet, result in conditions that may be connected to AD, including obesity, diabetes, high blood pressure, and heart disease. As Snowdon determined in his study of nuns, a good diet and exercise, not smoking, and keeping active are important in maintaining the kind of healthy lifestyle that may prevent AD, as are education and continuing to be a lifelong learner.

CARING FOR AD PATIENTS

Caring for a loved one with AD is demanding and exhausting. Many books address strategies for everyday living as an AD caregiver.

Here are some pointers that family members should keep in mind when dealing with a person who has dementia:

- Do not talk down to the person or treat him or her like a child. Such expressions as "Do we want our sweater?" is not what one would say to an adult.
- Conversation may be difficult. A person with AD may ask the same question several times; they have not remembered they asked the question.
- Do not become impatient. Do not let your non-verbal gestures or expression show disgust or annoyance.
- When giving directions, talk slowly. Writing down reminders may help. Although AD impairs reading and writing skills, the person may remember after re-reading a note several times.
- Keep sentences short and simple. Do not give too much information at one time.
- Do not argue with the person. You will not win. One caregiver told how her mother said she found her in a basket in the yard. The caregiver responded, "Yes, it was crowded in that basket." Her mother never mentioned the basket again.
- Respect the dignity of the people with AD. They may be ill with a terrible condition, but they are still human beings.

People with AD sometimes react with aggression and anger, even lashing out at the caregiver. Jacqueline Marcel, a writer and speaker, told how she cared for two parents with AD. Her mother was frail and passive, but her father was difficult. Sometimes he was passive and charming, but at other times, he was violent and angry. Her book, *Elder Rage, or Take My Father . . . Please*, describes how she used proper medications, tough love, and behavior modification to help her 85-year-old father.

One part of her book discusses what happens to the mind affected by AD. The areas of the brain that produce aggressive behavior are the frontal lobe, the temporal lobe, and the limbic system. The limbic system is sometimes referred to as the oldest, most primitive part of the brain. When any of these brain areas are damaged, the person may display impulsive, emotional, or out-of-context responses. Damage to areas below the cortex, such as the hypothalamus or brainstem, may result in sudden outbursts. The person may spit, pound, bite, or kick. Medications are often necessary to control aggression, but they must be the proper medication given by a physician specializing in treating the disease.

This chapter has focused on present treatments for AD. Chapter 8 looks at research that is being done that addresses the underlying causes of the disease.

8

THE FUTURE OF ALZHEIMER'S DISEASE

The miniature doctors navigated their tiny submarine through the dangerous passages of the arteries, **capillaries**, and veins. Their goal was to dissolve a blood clot in the patient's brain. Along the way, they met the killer white blood cells that protect the body from outside invaders. This plot, from the 1966 film *Fantastic Voyage*, is fantasy, but some of the treatments that are cutting edge today are more amazing than science fiction. Certain new drug therapies, vaccines, stem cell research, gene therapy, and nanotechnology are once-futuristic ideas that scientists now see as successful treatments.

Without a treatment, the future for AD appears bleak. The Alzheimer's Association projects that there will be 16 million people with AD by 2050. Medicare (the government health care program for people over age 65) and Medicaid (the government health care program for those under the poverty level) spend billions of dollars a year on patients with AD. With the aging of the baby boom generation, the large group of people born between 1945 and 1964, these costs are expected to triple.

NEW DRUG THERAPIES

Many companies are conducting research to develop new drug therapies for AD. Scientists expect to find some effective therapies within the next 10 years, if not sooner. Nine new drugs for AD are in Phase III of clinical trials, the final stage before FDA approval. An additional 23 drugs are in Phase II. Many of these drugs are not just temporary treatments that stall the disease, but are remedies that target the genetic pathways of the disease to prevent AD or prevent further damage in a person already sufferng from AD.

Two drugs are close to approval:

- Flurizan is a drug that reduces levels of β-amyloid in cultured human cells and animal models. Results from a completed Phase II study in July 2006 show that Flurizan actually modifies the disease. The longer the patients were treated, the more slowly their disease progressed. Phase III results are expected in the summer of 2008.
- Alzhemed is thought to reduce β-amyloid by binding to it. The positive Phase II results were presented in a scientific journal in November 2006. Now Alzhemed is undergoing two large trials in the United States and Europe.

The Roskamp Institute in Sarasota, Florida, has identified more than 300 compounds that can lower amyloid in mice. The scientists at Roskamp take drugs that are known to be safe for humans and tweak them chemically until they lower amyloid. Then the question arises: Will the compound that is so effective in the test tube and in mice work in humans? Many of the drugs that are effective in mice fail human tests, because the human system does not work exactly like the mouse system.

PERSONALIZED MEDICINE

The sequencing of the human genome, first published in 2001, has led to progress in understanding the molecular basis of disease. A new field of medicine called pharmacogenomics is expected to usher in a new age of treatment. Pharmacogenomics combines the word *pharmaco*, meaning drugs, with the word *genomics*, the study of genes and their function. In pharmacogenomics, scientists study the interaction between the genetic makeup of the patient and his or her response to a drug. Using this information, the researcher gives the right dose of the right drug to the right patient at the right time. In a disease such as AD, where tolerance of therapy often determines success, pharmacogenomics offers promise. This powerful tool for finding drug targets offers help in improving the practical side of patient care.

A VACCINE FOR AD

Early in 2000, enthusiasm was high for a potential vaccine for AD. Mice had responded to a compound called AN1792. Plaques disappeared and the mice began to respond in normal ways. Elan Corporation, an Irish company, was in Phase II trials with human subjects. Then 18 of the 300 participants contracted meningoencephalitis, an inflammation of the brain and spinal cord. The trial was stopped immediately.

Such problems do arise in cutting-edge research. Elan, however, did not stop working with the findings. The researchers wanted to analyze what had happened. After analysis, they found that some patients—but not all—made antibodies to the β-amyloid peptide. Questions still remain as to what caused the inflammation. Because the immune system varies in each person, different people responded in different ways to this vaccine. The investigators now believe a subset of people can benefit from immunization. Elan has re-grouped its research and is hopeful that the vaccine will be a future possibility.

STEM CELL RESEARCH

Stem cell research is a topic that is often in the news. Many of the stories focus on the possibility of what can be done with stem cells; other stories discuss the controversy surrounding them.

What are stem cells? Three important features characterize them:

- They are unspecialized cells that can renew themselves for long periods through cell division. "Unspecialized" means that stem cells have the potential to develop into different kinds of cells.
- Under certain conditions, stem cells can be stimulated to develop into bone, blood, or nerve cells, or other specialized cells.
- Genes control how stem cells can give rise to specialized cells. Other chemicals, such as growth factors, can be used to determine what type of cells form from stem cells.

There are several sources of stem cells: Embryonic stem cells, derived from an embryo; embryonic germ stem cells, derived from an egg or sperm; and adult stem cells, derived from tissue that has already been specialized. The most controversial are the embryonic stem cells, because the embryo must be destroyed to harvest them.

In animal models, stem cells have been stimulated to become neurons and glial cells. Mice that have had chemically stimulated stem cells directly injected into the brain can produce functional neurons near the areas of the plaques

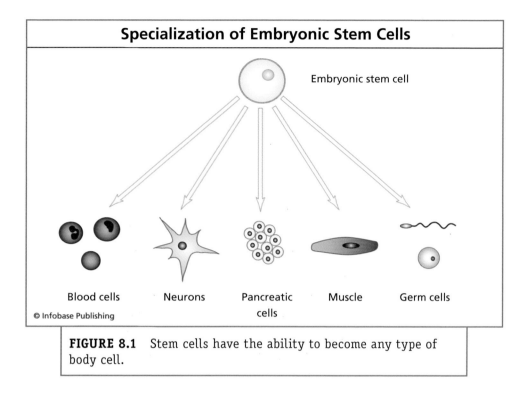

FIGURE 8.1   Stem cells have the ability to become any type of body cell.

and tangles. It is not known yet whether these neurons will make the correct connections and be able to replace the complex damage caused by AD. Currently, there are no human trials using stem cells.

GENE THERAPY AND AD

Gene therapy is a rapidly growing field of medicine. Many people consider gene therapy to be the future answer to many human diseases and disorders, including AD. The idea of the procedure seems simple: insert a normal gene into a person's cells or tissues to replace a faulty gene. It is much like a transplant. Although transplanting an organ like a heart or kidney is very complex, inserting genes involves thousands of small molecules that cannot be seen even with the most powerful microscopes.

Actually, gene therapy is more similar to a conventional medical treatment than may seem at first glance. Instead of treating the disease with a drug or with surgery, doctors treat the patient with DNA. Gene therapy uses **recombinant DNA** technology. Recombinant DNA refers to a form of DNA produced by splicing together segments of DNA from different sources.

How is gene therapy administered? Genes cannot be taken like a pill. They must be inserted into the cell's nucleus. In the 1960s, scientists realized that viruses enter cells and then use the cell's own DNA to produce more viruses. Scientists developed the ability to cut out the infectious part of the viral genome and insert the genes to be transferred into the viral DNA. This produces a virus that still has the ability to get into the body's cells, but that does not cause infection. The virus carries the desired genes into the cells.

In gene therapy, the normal genes are isolated from a normal chromosome. The genes are then attached to the DNA of harmless viruses. When injected into the body, the viruses carrying the normal gene enter the cells; there, they replicate like normal viruses and deliver the gene to the cell. These viruses are called **vectors**, meaning carriers.

Scientists currently have several approaches for correcting a defect via recombinant DNA:

◆ Gene insertion. A normal gene is put into the genome to replace a gene that is not working. This is the most common approach.
◆ Gene modification. The mutant gene is swapped for a normal gene.
◆ Gene surgery. The abnormal gene is repaired so that it functions normally.

◆ Gene regulation. The process that controls or regulates the gene is turned off or on, depending on the desired results.

Alzheimer's disease researchers at the Salk Institute in California are experimenting with mouse memory. The scientists reduced the amount of an important enzyme that cuts the amyloid precursor protein (APP) and releases toxic fragments. The mouse models were in an advanced stage of the disease. After treatment, the mice were able to function normally. They remembered how to eat and even how to run mazes. Inactivation of this enzyme could be important in the treatment of Alzheimer's disease in humans.

In 2005, a team of scientists from the University of California, San Diego used the first gene therapy treatment for a patient with AD. First, they harvested and processed skin cells from the patient. They then inserted the gene that directs the production of a protein called **nerve growth factor (NGF).** NGF is a naturally occurring protein in normal brains that keeps cells alive and growing. Surgeons injected 2.5 million genetically modified cells into the frontal lobe of the brain. After two years, PET scans of patients undergoing this treatment showed increased activity in the harvested cells. The patients continued to have memory loss, but at a much slower rate than before gene therapy. This was a successful Phase I study for safety.

In another gene therapy treatment released in 2005, Dr. Roy Bakay and a team at Rush University in Chicago injected 40 billion viruses into six patients with mild to moderate AD. The researchers used the following procedure:

◆ First, they stripped genetic material from viruses and inserted the gene for NFG, which keeps memory cells alive.

◆ They injected the 40 billion viruses into the forebrain through holes drilled on either side of the
upper skull.

◆ The vector viruses released DNA into the nucleus
of the memory cells.

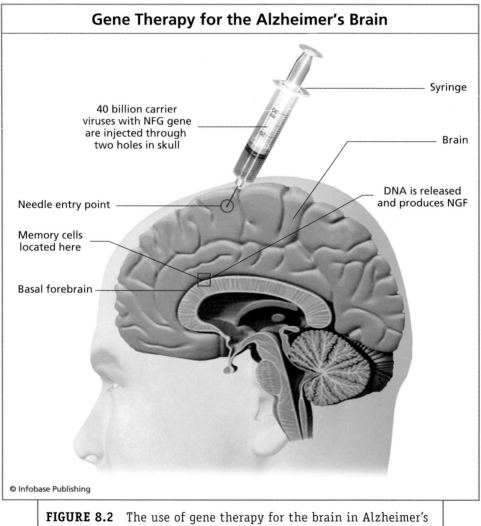

Gene Therapy for the Alzheimer's Brain

Syringe

40 billion carrier
viruses with NFG gene
are injected through
two holes in skull

Brain

DNA is released
and produces NGF

Needle entry point

Memory cells
located here

Basal forebrain

© Infobase Publishing

FIGURE 8.2 The use of gene therapy for the brain in Alzheimer's
disease patients resulted in success in some patients.

♦ The DNA produced NGF, which was released to the rest of the brain to maintain cells important to memory.

♦ Results indicated success in some patients.

Gene therapy remains a cutting-edge procedure. There are still questions about how well it works and ethical questions such as where to draw the line between medical treatment and optional enhancement. It will likely be 10 to 20 years before gene therapy can become a widespread medical procedure.

NANOTECHNOLOGY

In 1959, Richard Feynman gave a speech called "There's Plenty of Room at the Bottom" to an audience of scientists. He asked the question: What would happen if we could arrange atoms one by one in any way we want? He suggested starting with atoms and then building the structures that we want from them. With that challenge, scientists began to explore the world of nanotechnology.

Nano is the Greek word meaning "one-billionth" of something. That something can be a second, a liter, or a meter. To avoid all the zeroes, scientists write it as 10^{-9}. Nanotechnology encompasses a world of very tiny things. With the tools of nanotechnology, one could print all the pages of Encyclopedia Britannica on the head of a pin.

In 2006, researchers in Chile found that adding gold nanostructures dissolved the β-amyloid clumps of AD. The clumps failed to reform even after several weeks. These experiments were done in a test tube, but plans are being made for animal studies. If successful, this nanotechnology treatment could prove effective at treating the plaques of AD.

In 1986, scientist K. Eric Drexler wrote *Engines of Creation: The Coming Era of Nanotechnology*. In this futuristic book, Drexler describes how nanotechnology could create a state of health, not just treat disease. According to Drexler, the coming age will be the "Age of Nanomedicine." Drexler maintains that aging, illness, and injury cause scrambled or misarranged atoms. If scientists can find out how to correct misarranged atoms, they can then rebuild them one at a time. They could even rebuild the damage caused by the plaques and tangles of AD.

Nanomedical devices would include nanorobots and quantum devices that would repair conditions in a fashion similar to the submarine in the *Fantastic Voyage*.

The future of pharmocogenomics, vaccines, stem cells, gene therapy, and nanotechnology is promising. Although many of the ideas that are advanced today will never reach clinical and practical applications, it will take only a few breakthroughs to revolutionize the way brain diseases are treated and prevented. In addition to problems of determining how best to use these technologies, many of these cutting-edge procedures pose questions of ethics in research. Chapter 9 considers some of these ethical questions.

9

ETHICAL ISSUES OF A BRAVE NEW WORLD

The students are amazed at what they see in the nursery. Their teacher has assigned them to write a report on an exciting new method of research. The nursery is called a Hatchery. The professor at the Hatchery explains that the goal is to produce thousands of identical human embryos. The embryos will then be programmed to become citizens of a brave new world, based on science.

The professor continues to explain that as the embryos pass along a conveyor belt, they will be classified into five groups. They will be chosen at random to become Alphas, Betas, Gammas, Deltas, or Epsilons. Alpha and Beta embryos will be cultivated into people of the highest intellectual and physical stature, with Gammas, Deltas, and Epsilons being suppressed into followers. Alpha embryos will become the leaders of the World State. The Epsilons are deprived of oxygen so that their minds are stunted; they will be menial workers of the state. As infants, the Deltas will receive a shock anytime they reach for any beautiful thing, such as a flower or a book; they will never question anything and will become easily led. There will be more Deltas than other groups.

In this manner, Aldous Huxley opens his 1932 novel *Brave New World.* Such books may agitate distrust of science. On the other hand, they warn that research in the wrong hands can lead to disaster. Chapter 8 of this book considered the future of AD research. While pharmacogenomics, stem cell research, gene therapy, and nanotechnology hold great promise, there are ethical concerns about their use as treatments.

This chapter explores ethical issues relating especially to AD research. It begins with the Hippocratic Oath, which states that doctors must never prescribe a procedure that may harm a patient. The Nuremberg code of 1947 and the Belmont report of 1979 established patients' rights and the principles for human medical experimentation. These documents first developed the idea of **informed consent**, which means the patient must understand what will happen in an experiment and must agree in writing. Information must be presented to patients in words that they can understand, and they cannot be forced into signing.

Other ethical issues relating to AD involve participating in cutting-edge research, such as stem cell research and gene therapy, whose remaining unknowns and complexity make it difficult to explain to a patient for his or her consent. Some practical items, such as genetic testing and counseling for the relatives of people with AD, confidentiality issues, and assisted suicide, are addressed in this chapter.

FIRST DO NO HARM

The foundations of the treatment of AD patients began on the tiny island of Cos off the coast of Greece. According to legend, Asclepius, the god of medicine, settled his son Podalirius on the island to become a healer. Superstition and ritual were parts of medical treatment. For example, in ancient Greece, healers would make the patient sleep on a hard cave floor at night, and his or her treatment would be determined from his or her dream. The healer would interpret the dream and prescribe the treatment, which often was harsh and unreasonable. Treatments were prescribed even when the patient had no chance of recovering.

The physician Hippocrates, born on Cos around 460 B.C., disagreed with these superstitions. He gave treatments that were gentle, simple, and often effective. He wrote his ideals in a paper that pledged, "I will give no deadly medicine to anyone if asked, nor suggest any such counsel." Those words became part of the oath that graduating physicians take today, the Hippocratic Oath.

Due to medical advances during the twentieth century, scientists realized that laboratory rats and guinea pig research could go only so far. They knew that it would become necessary to try experimental procedures on human beings. Some experiments were done on people without their knowing it. Many people died. Concerned with this drastic abuse of medicine, some people concerned with the ethics of research began to assert that each person had the right to decide whether they wanted to participate in research. To treat people as rats or guinea pigs was unethical. A person should not be used in trials unless the experiment would benefit that person.

What does this have to do with AD? Using what knowledge is available, physicians must give people with AD the best care possible. Yet AD is a condition for which there is no known cure. Human subjects are necessary in order to test potential cures, some of which may hold significant risks for the patient. What if a human subject receives a drug for AD that proves not to be safe?

Ethicists are people who study issues of what is right and wrong. Medical ethicists look at situations in light of medical experiments; they are usually part of the staff of major research universities. Some ethicists believe that people

FIGURE 9.1 Hippocrates, who lived around 460 to 377 B.C., was a medical practitioner who is considered the father of Western medicine and the person responsible for the ethical standard known as the Hippocratic Oath.

should not be used in trials without their knowledge, but add that if the person agrees to participate willingly in medical research and understands what the consequences may be, human experimentation is ethical.

HUMAN EXPERIMENTATION AND INFORMED CONSENT

Informed consent is a result of the ethical principle of "respect for persons." The person is told about all possible risks and benefits of a procedure. He or she then considers the intent, action, and consequences and makes a personal decision.

The idea of informed consent came about in the second half of the twentieth century. In 1900, the Berlin Code described ethical conditions for human medical research. When Adolph Hitler came to power in Germany in 1933, however, he said that this code did not apply to certain groups, and that Jews, gypsies, and people with mental disabilities, such as dementia, had no rights. This decree opened the door for the atrocities that took place in Nazi concentration camps under the guise of medical research.

In the aftermath of World War II, responding to the horrors that Nazi doctors had performed in the name of medicine, doctors and government officials developed the Nuremberg Code, which demanded researchers meet 10 conditions of ethical research. In 1979, in the United States, the Belmont Report incorporated some of these principles and introduced the following critieria for ethical research:

◆ Respect for persons.
◆ Beneficence. All research must aim to maximize benefit and minimize risk.

◆ Justice. Those involved in medical research must never injure one person to benefit another.

◆ Informed consent. Each person must be informed in writing and receive information in a language that the individual can understand.

◆ Risk/benefit assessment. Few people would volunteer if they thought they would die. Independent committees must be established to determine risk to patients. Risk and benefit may be thought of as a scale. The risk or possible danger must be weighed against the possible benefit.

◆ Selection of subjects must be fair. High-risk experiments must not be performed on just one type of population, such as prisoners or low-income groups.

FIGURE 9.2 The actor Michael J. Fox is a supporter of stem cell research. Fox, who suffers from Parkinson's disease, believes that stem cell research can lead to cures for many genetic diseases.

One can see a potential problem here for AD research. The person with AD must understand that he or she is part of an experimental procedure, yet that may be difficult to do if the person has cognitive impairment. Thus, this type of subject could not be accepted under the rules of ethical research.

Understanding how research works is essential to grasp ethical issues. Research protocols are often set up as double-blind, placebo experiments. A **placebo** is an inactive substance that has the same form as the medication but is completely inactive. A **double-blind experiment** is one in which both the people who are taking the drug and the people who are administering the trials do not know who is receiving the treatment and who is receiving the placebo. Sometimes the effects of a new drug are compared with a standard treatment instead of a placebo. In order for the patient to be fully informed, he or she must understand the nature of the experiment, including whether placebo or standard treatment may be used.

CUTTING-EDGE EXPERIMENTS

Cutting-edge research using stem cells and gene therapy has its own set of problems. The science behind these procedures is complex and difficult to explain in general. Explaining the research to people with dementia is even more difficult. One of the problems is that some people will agree to participate in research without fully understanding what they are doing. The researcher must not pressure and must not accept the patient if he or she suspects the patient does not understand the conditions of the study.

The FDA, NIH, and a panel of 21 experts called the Recombinant DNA Advisory Committee (RAC) carefully monitor cutting-edge human experiments. Since the death of Jesse

Gelsinger in a gene therapy experiment in 1999, the FDA, NIH, and RAC have put major demands upon any experiments in this area. Another highly publicized death like that of Jesse Gelsinger could end further human experimentation in gene therapy.

In addition to major safety issues, there are other concerns about gene therapy. There are concerns about the re-engineering of viruses and the possibility of inadvertantly creating a new infectious disease. Some of the sensational stories created by news media do not help this perception. Barbara Walters hosted a TV program that featured the possibility of a brave new world of perfect designer people

THE DEATH OF JESSE GELSINGER

In 1999, on his eighteenth birthday, Jesse Gelsinger and his family headed from their Arizona home to Philadelphia. They went to the University of Pennsylvania, where Jesse signed up to participate in a gene-therapy experiment to correct an inherited condition called ornithine transcarbamylase (OTC) deficiency. OTC causes the body to build up deadly levels of ammonia.

Jesse had been lucky. Most children with the disorder live only a month. But Jesse had only a partial condition, and with several days of intensive care and a change of medication, he had survived each attack. He was tired of these treatments and was excited to sign up for a new gene-therapy experiment to improve his own health and to help others.

Four months later, on September 17, 1999, Jesse died. The gene-therapy treatment involved injecting a normal OTC gene attached to a virus into his liver. Within hours, his temperature shot up, his blood began clotting, ammonia levels climbed, his created by genetic engineering. **Eugenics** was a movement in the early part of the twentieth century that promoted the idea that only those with desirable genes should reproduce. Such an idea could exclude people with known genetic diseases, mental disabilities, and physical disorders. Could gene therapy lead to a new form of eugenics?

In dealing with these cutting-edge experiments, several other ethical issues emerge:

◆   What diseases should be treated? Should only fatal diseases be treated or all diseases, such as the common cold? Should the diseases be ones

liver hemorrhaged, and a flood of white blood cells shut down his lungs. Jesse's death was the first gene-therapy fatality.

A storm of ethical questions about the gene therapy raged. Did the University of Pennsylvania explain the risks to Jesse? Was there a problem with the quality of informed consent at the university? Did the university not report toxic effects in animals that could have shut down the study? Did the researchers possibly profit from the use of their own vectors, which they bought from their own private company? Were the researchers concerned about their own power and prestige? When reports of 650 adverse reactions from other gene-therapy experiments throughout the country emerged, the FDA stopped gene-therapy experiments.

What went wrong? The Gelsinger disaster was to gene therapy as the Columbia shuttle disaster was to NASA. The researchers had to stop all activity to find out what happened and then regroup to correct it. Gene therapy is slowly and cautiously regaining respect.

that have no other treatment? AD currently has no cure and might fit into the gene-therapy treatment category because it is always fatal.

- ◆ Who is chosen for the treatment, and who is not? Should only terminal patients be chosen or should it be those with moderate disease conditions? Some ethicists said that Jesse Gelsinger should never have been considered, because he was controlling his condition with drugs.

- ◆ Should genes and stem cells be patented? Is it ethical for scientists who develop these procedures to patent them? Currently, genes can also be patented. The ethical question is: Should one person or university own a gene?

- ◆ Who will pay for these cutting edge procedures? Currently, insurance will not pay for gene therapy. A gene-therapy procedure may cost as much as $500,000 per patient. Will only the rich be able to afford this type of medical care?

- ◆ Should parents be able to choose the looks or abilities of their child? These choices are called cosmetic.

GENETIC TESTING

If you are carrying a gene for a serious disease that might show up later in life, would you want to know? This is the question that many people find themselves facing when they realize a close relative has AD and they might also be at risk.

A blood test is available to identify *APOE* alleles. *APOE* is already associated with heart disease, which is a well-studied condition. The blood test cannot tell people whether they will develop AD or when. All it does is give a yes-or-no answer to the presence of the allele. Some people want to know whether they will get AD in later life. This type of prediction is not possible yet. *APOE* tests will probably never be able to do this with 100% accuracy.

Genetic testing for AD is available under very specific circumstances. Because only one gene causes the early-onset form, genetic testing for healthy people may be done. In some cases, testing can confirm AD in people who already show the symptoms. Mutations in the single genes *APP*, *PS-1*, and *PS-2* cause AD. If one of a person's parents has these genes, there is a 50% chance that he or she will inherit them. A genetics counselor can assess the person's risk of carrying one of these mutations and determine whether genetic testing is appropriate.

Mutations in *APP*, *PS-1*, and *PS-2* indicate the person will develop the disease. The fourth gene *APOE* is also an indicator of risk, but does not guarantee the disease. This is the main reason for not testing for *APOE*. In a research setting, *APOE* testing is valuable for identifying study volunteers who may be at risk of developing AD. Researchers can look for brain changes in the volunteers, using noninvasive diagnostic tests. These tests could also be used to compare the effectiveness of treatments for patients with different *APOE* statuses. *APOE* is valuable in studying large groups of healthy people. In 1995, a group of scientists, ethicists, and health professionals wrote a public policy about *APOE* testing and genetic counseling for AD. Importantly, the policy states that tests should not be used to predict AD.

Should families receive genetic counseling? There are pros and cons to the issue. Remember that the *APOE* gene does not doom one to having the disease. Likewise, a person may develop AD without having the gene. The general policy is that until there are more effective preventative or curative treatments for AD, genetic counseling is not a good idea for most people. Predictive screening in otherwise healthy people will be useful when effective ways to treat or prevent AD are available.

CONCERNS ABOUT CONFIDENTIALITY

APOE testing and all genetic testing raise ethical, legal, and social questions for which there are few answers. Confidentiality laws protect information gathered for research. On the other hand, information obtained from *APOE* tests may not be protected as confidential if it is part of a person's medical records. Employers, insurance companies, and other health care organizations could potentially gain access to this information, and discrimination could result. For example, employment opportunities and long-term care insurance premiums could be affected for a person who is known to be an eventual AD patient. Little is known about how widely stigma associated with increased risk for AD may affect individuals and their families.

ETHICAL ISSUE: ASSISTED SUICIDE

The issue of **euthanasia,** or assisted suicide, is certainly controversial. The word *euthanasia* comes from two Greek words: *eu* meaning "good" or "well," and *thanatos* meaning "death." Euthanasia carries the idea of a painless death for the good of the individual. Those who promote euthanasia consider it to be a reasonable approach to help a person in unbearable pain.

The Netherlands has allowed euthanasia for more than 30 years. The country has guidelines to protect people from abuse, but many people question whether these guidelines are carefully enforced. Recently the Dutch government has opened the legal door to permit euthanasia for patients with AD. In a book, *Dancing with Mr. D.*, Dutch nursing-home doctor Bert Keizer describes how he gave lethal injections. Most of his euthanized cases were not in pain but were frail, elderly people. The Dutch Parliament is also considering legalizing death for infants and children who may have certain harmful disorders.

The state of Oregon passed an assisted-suicide law in 1997. An article in the Portland *Oregonian* reported that doctors said most of the patients do not seek death because of pain, but because they fear being a burden and fear losing dignity. Other state governments including Washington state, Vermont, and California are currently considering similar provisions. People who support euthanasia argue the costs involved. Drugs used for suicide cost about $100. To take care of a person with AD could cost more than $100,000.

Opponents of assisted suicide believe such laws will lead to a slippery slope of disregard for human rights. They point to an Oregon case in which a woman with Alzheimer's disease and cancer received euthanasia even after her psychiatrist said that she had no idea what she was asking for and that her daughter was the driving force behind the request. Issues such as greed for insurance money and inheritance might lead to elder abuse.

Many in opposition consider assisted suicide murder. They point to the ethical concept that human beings must be treated with dignity. Places such as **hospice** organizations care for the dying with dignity.

Ethicists attack euthanasia in general as a violation of the principle of "first do not harm," the provision of the Hippocratic Oath. A doctor must not permit harm to come to the person, and death may certainly be considered harm.

The ethical issues surrounding AD are many, including issues of what constitutes informed consent, the value of genetic testing, and the morality of assisted suicide. These are important because human beings have differing beliefs about the nature of life. Initiatives for assisted suicide and euthanasia will probably appear on ballots in more states. Even if prevention and successful treatments for AD are found, the ethical questions will continue.

GLOSSARY

Allele   One form of a gene at a given location along a chromosome.

Alzheimer's disease   A condition in which the brain slowly shrivels and dies.

Amino acid   A small organic molecule that is a building block of proteins.

Arteries   The blood vessels that carry blood with oxygen away from the heart to all parts of the body.

Apolipoprotein epsilon (*APOE*)   A gene located on chromosome 19; it has three alleles and is associated with late-onset AD.

Autopsy   The procedure performed to determine the cause of death.

Axons   A long fiber extending from the cell body of a neuron; it carries impulses away from the cell body.

Capillaries   The smallest blood vessels that connect arteries and veins; the sites of exchange of oxygen, carbon dioxide, nutrients, and wastes between the blood and the cells of the body.

Cloning   Copying a fragment of DNA.

Cell body   the central command center of the neuron that contains the nucleus and various cell organelles. The axon and dendrites conduct electrical signals to and from the cell body.

Cell membrane The structure that surrounds the cell and controls the movement of substances into and out of the cell.

Cerebrum The part of the brain located in the front of the skull that is the site of all consciousness, thought processes, and voluntary movement.

Chromosomes Colored bodies found in the nucleus of the cell that contain DNA.

Codon A triplet of messenger RNA that specifies a particular amino acid.

Cognition The ability to think, reason, and use proper judgment.

Computed tomography (CT scan) A machine that produces three-dimensional X-ray images.

Cytoplasm The material that fills the cell between the nucleus and cell membrane; contains many tiny structures called organelles.

Dementia A broad impairment of intellectual function that is usually progressive and that interferes with normal social and occupational activities.

Dendrites Branchlike extensions from the body of the nerve cell; they carry impulses from neighboring nerve cells toward the cell body.

Deoxyribonucleic acid (DNA) A long molecule in the form of a twisted ladder; consists of sugars, phosphate groups, and four different nitrogen-containing bases.

Diabetes A disease in which there is either inadequate amounts of insulin—the hormone that regulates sugar in the blood—or the cells of the body cannot use the insulin normally; insulin is made in the pancreas.

Dominant trait   A trait that appears whenever the gene is present in the genome, even one copy of the gene.

Double-blind experiment   An experiment in which researchers do not know who is receiving the experimental treatment and who is receiving a placebo.

Early-onset AD   A rare form of Alzheimer's disease that affects people younger than age 65.

Electrocardiograph (EKG)   A machine that shows the electrical activity of the heart.

Electroencephalograph (EEG)   A machine that shows the electrical activity of the brain.

Enzymes   Proteins that speed up the chemical reactions in living organisms; the enzymes are regenerated unchanged at the end of the reactions.

Ethicists   People who study issues of what is right and wrong.

Eugenics   A movement in the early part of the twentieth century that supported the idea that only those with desirable genes should reproduce.

Euthanasia   From the Greek words "eu" and "thanatos," meaning a good or painless death.

Familial Alzheimer's disease (FAD)   A rare form of Alzheimer's disease that is inheritable. Symptoms can occur as early as age 40.

Functional magnetic resonance imaging (fMRI)   A type of magnetic resonance imaging that allows the researcher to see functioning of the brain as it reacts.

Gene   A sequence of DNA that instructs a cell to produce a particular protein.

Genetics   The study of how traits are passed on from one generation to the next.

Genome   The entire complement of DNA in an organism.

Geriatrician   A person who studies and treats diseases of older adults.

Hippocampus   A structure located deep in the brain that is thought to be a control center for memory; shaped like a seahorse.

Hospice   An organization that cares for the dying.

Human Genome Project   Program to decode the complete human genome; the project was completed in 2003.

Informed consent   A written agreement stating that a patient understands the risks of a treatment. The information explaining the proposed treatment must be in clear language.

Late-onset AD   The most common form of Alzheimer's disease, which affects people over age 65.

Magnetic resonance imaging (MRI)   A medical procedure that uses a magnetic field to create a detailed, multi-level image of the brain.

Medicare   The government health program for Americans age 65 and older.

Mendelian laws   Laws of heredity named for Gregor Mendel; the laws describe the inheritance patterns for simple dominant and recessive traits.

Molecular biology   The study of cell activities at molecular and atomic levels.

Mutation   A change in a gene's biochemical makeup; a change in DNA.

National Institute on Aging (NIA)   A federal agency that provides biomedical, social, and behavioral research on aging.

Nerve growth factor (NGF)   A naturally occurring protein that keeps nerve cells alive and growing.

Nervous system   Body system that comprises the brain, spinal cord, and nerves.

Neurofibrillary tangles (NFTs)   Nerve fibers in the brain that appear tangled under the microscope; an indication of AD.

Neurology   The study of the nervous system and its diseases.

Neuron   A nerve cell.

Neurotransmitter   A chemical released by an axon ending; it crosses a synapse and stimulates impulses in a neighboring neuron.

Nucleotides   The building blocks of DNA and RNA; consist of a nitrogen-containing base, a sugar molecule, and a phosphate molecule.

Nucleus   The central part of a cell that regulates all of the cell's activities.

Organelles   Small structures located in the cytoplasm of a cell.

Placebo   In an experiment, an inactive substance that does not contain medication, but that has the same form as the medication.

Plaques   Deposits of β-amyloid, which appear as clumps and are found in the brains of people with AD at autopsy.

Polymerase chain reaction (PCR)   A procedure used to create multiple copies of a piece of DNA.

Positron emission tomography (PET)   A type of imaging that uses nuclear tracing devices to create pictures.

Precursor   A building block.

Protein   A type of molecule consisting of amino acids linked together; the direct product of genetic information.

Proteome   All of the proteins in the human body.

Quantitative trait loci   Stretches of DNA that are closely linked to the genes that underlie the trait in question.

Recessive trait   A trait whose presence is masked by another, dominant trait.

Recombinant DNA   DNA molecules in which a sequence that is not normally in the DNA is placed into the molecule.

Restriction enzymes   Enzymes that cut DNA in certain places.

Ribonucleic acid (RNA)   A nucleic acid whose sequence of building blocks represents a gene's sequence or that assists in protein synthesis.

Risk   The possibility that certain factors will cause a disease or disorder.

Senile   The term is from the Latin word meaning "old"; however, in the nineteenth century, it became related to progressive decline as one ages; the term is not used now.

Sex chromosomes   The pair of chromosomes that contain the genes that distinguish the sexes; females have two X chromosomes, and males have one X and one Y chromosome.

Somatic chromosomes   The autosomes; the 22 pairs of chromosomes other than the sex chromosomes.

Sundown syndrome   The symptom that describes agitation and wandering that occurs regularly in the late afternoon in AD patients.

Synapse   The gap between neurons.

Translation   The process by which the information in mRNA is used in protein synthesis.

Transcription   The transfer of information from one strand of DNA to mRNA.

Vector   A carrier.

Veins   Blood vessels that carry blood laden with carbon dioxide from the body's cells back to the lungs.

Ventricles   Areas or spaces in the brain that appear enlarged in those with AD.

BIBLIOGRAPHY

"Alzheimer's Approved Drugs." Fisher Center for Alzheimer's Research Web site. URL: http://www.alzinfo.org/alzheimers-treatment-cognitive.asp. Accessed March 5, 2007.

Bertram, Lars, et al. "Systematic meta-analysis of Alzheimer disease genetic association studies: The AlzGene database." *Nature Genetics* 39 (2007): 17–23.

"Bioethics: Gene Therapy business and the tragic case of Jesse Gelsinger." News Weekly Web site. URL: http://www.newsweekly.com.au/articles/2000aug12_bio.html Accessed September 12, 2006.

Bren, Linda. "Alzheimer's: Searching for a Cure." U.S. Food and Drug Administration Web site. URL: http://www.fda.gov/fdac/features/2003/403_alz.html. Accessed September, 27, 2006.

Brower, Vicki. "The Genetics of Aging." *Genetic Engineering News* 22 (2002): 1 and 61.

Bumiller, Elizabeth. "Effects of Reagan Illness Detailed," *Boston Globe*, June 8, 1995: 3.

"David Snowden 3/23/04." Alzheimer's Association Web site. URL: http://www.alz.org/join_the_cause_david_snowden_32304.asp. Accessed March 1, 2007.

"Decoding Alzheimer's." BusinessWeek Web site. URL: http://www.businessweek.com/magazine/content/07_02/b4016060.htm?chan=top%2Bnews. Accessed March 4, 2007.

Fackelman, Kathleen. "The Race Against Alzheimer's." *The Dana Foundation's Brain in the News* 11 (2004): 1–2.

Gandhi, Unnati. "Diabetes Research Could Aid in Alzheimer's Fight." *The Dana Foundation's Brain in the News* 13 (2006): 1–2.

Gatz, M., et al. "Role of genes and environments for explaining Alzheimer disease." *Archives of General Psychiatry* 63 (2006): 168–174.

"Genetics and Alzheimer's Disease." ElderCare Online Web site. URL: http://ec-online.net/Knowledge/articles/genetics.html. Accessed September, 27 2006.

Gillick, Muriel R. *Tangled Minds: Understanding Alzheimer's Disease and Other Dementias.* New York: Dutton, 1998.

Kelly, Evelyn B. *Confronting Alzheimer's Disease: Medical Progress and Coping Skills.* Tallahassee, FL: ArcMesa Educators, 1997. (a CME course for health professionals)

Lanza, Robert. *Handbook of Stem Cell Research*, Vol 1. Burlington MA: Elsevier, 2004.

"Law Enforcement Officer's Guide for Responding to Persons with Alzheimer's Disease." Tallahassee, FL: Alzheimer's Association, Florida Chapters, 2006.

Lewis, Ricki. *Human Genetics: Concepts and Applications.* Dubuque, IA: William C. Brown, 1997.

Liberman, Bruce. "Genetic Link is Identified for Aging, Alzheimer's." *The Dana Foundation's Brain in the News* 13 (2006): 1–2.

Lokvig, Jytte. *Alzheimer's A to Z: Secrets to Successful Caregiving.* Santa Fe, NM: Endless Circles Press, 2001.

Marcel, Jacqueline. *Elder Rage, or Take My Father Please!* Irvine, CA: Impressive Press, 2001.

Maurer, Konrad, and Ulrike Maurer. *Alzheimer: The Life of a Physician and the Career of a Disease.* New York: Columbia Press, 2003.

Murdoch, Iris. "Books and Writers." Available online. URL: http://www.kirjasto.sci.fi/imurdoch.htm. Accessed February 24, 2007.

Murray, Bruce. "Building Better People: The Truths and Myths of Gene Therapy." URL: http://www.facsnet.org/tools/sci_tech/biotek/gene.php3. Accessed September 9, 2006.

Nohlgren, Stephen. "Closing in on Alzheimer's." Tampabay.com Web site. URL: http://www.sptimes.com/2007/02/27/Lifetimes/Closing_in_on_Alzheim.shtml. Accessed March 1, 2007.

"Overview Medications for Alzheimer's." About.com: Alzheimers. Available online. URL: http://alzheimers.about.com/cs/treatmentoptions/a/Alz_drugs.htm. Accessed March 7, 2007.

Phillips, Shawn. "Deviancy to Mental Illness: Nineteenth-century Developments in the Care of the Mentally Ill." *Science and Its Times: Understanding the Social Significance of Scientific Discovery* 5 (2000): 311–313.

Porter, Roy. *The Greatest Benefit to Mankind: A Medical History of Humanity.* New York: W.W. Norton, 1998.

Ridley, Matt. *Genome: The Autobiography of a Species in 23 Chapters.* New York: Perennial, 2000.

Sannes, Lucy. "Companies Spring Toward Alzheimer's Disease-modifying Drug." Cambridge Healthtech Institute Web site. URL: http://www.healthtech.com/news/strategic_briefings/2007/alzheimers.asp. Accessed March 5, 2007.

"Scientists Find New Genetic Clue to Cause of Alzheimer's Disease." NIH National Institute on Aging Web site. January 14, 2007. URL:http://www.nia.nih.gov/Alzheimers/ResearchInformation/NewsReleases/PR20070114SO/RL1gene.htm. Accessed March 4, 2007.

Shakespeare, William. *As You Like It*, II: vii.

Smith, Wesley J. "Assisted Suicide is Bad Medicine." *The Seattle Times* Web site. URL: http://seattletimes.nwsource.com/html/opinion/2002895854_wesleysmith29.html. Accessed March 18, 2007.

Srikameswaran, Anita. "Pittsburgh Compound Helps Track Alzheimer's." *The Dana Foundation's Brain in the News* 11 (2004): 1–2.

"Symptoms of Alzheimer's." Alzheimer's Association Web site. URL: http://www.alz.org/alzheimers_disease_symptoms_of_alzheimers.asp. Accessed March 4, 2007.

Tanzi, Rudolph. *The Molecular Genetics of Alzheimer's Disease.* Charlestown, MA: Massachusetts General Hospital, 2005.

"What We Know, What We Don't Know." Alzforum Web site. URL: http://www.alzforum.org/res/for/journal/centennial/whatweknow/whatweknow.asp.

FURTHER READING

Altman, Linda Jacobs. *Alzheimer's Disease.* Farmington Hills, MI: Thompson Gale, 2000.

Brill, Marlene Targ. *Alzheimer's Disease.* Tarrytown, NY: Marshall Cavendish, 2004.

Landau, Elaine. *Alzheimer's Disease: A Forgotten Life.* New York: Scolastic Library Publications, 2005.

Mace, Nancy L., and Peter V. Rabins. *The 36-Hour Day: A Family Guide to Caring for Persons with Alzheimer Disease, Related Dementing Illnesses, and Memory Loss in Later Life.* Baltimore: Johns Hopkins University Press, 1999.

McGuigan, Jim. *Alzheimer's Disease.* New York: Heineman, 2004.

Peterson, Ronald, ed. Mayo *Clinic on Alzheimer's Disease: Practical Answers to Memory Loss, Aging, Research, Treatment, and Caregiving.* Broomall, PA: Mason Crest Publishers, 2003.

Soliz, Adela. *Alzheimer's Disease.* Farmington Hills, MI: Thompson Gale, 2005.

Webber, Barbara. *Alzheimer's Disease.* Farmington Hills, MI: Thompson Gale, 2004.

Wright, Camron. *Letters to Emily.* New York: Simon & Schuster, 2006.

Fogarty, Mignon. "Genetic Testing for People Without Symptoms of Alzheimers." Genetic Health Web site. URL: http://www.genetichealth.com/ALZ_Genetics_Testing_in_Healthy_People.shtml. Accessed March 7, 2007.

WEB SITES

Alzheimer's Association
E-mail: info@alz.org
Web site: http://www.alz.org
Great resource for all kinds of information about AD

Alzheimer's Disease Education and Referral Center (ADEAR)
E-mail: adear@nia.nih.gov
Web site: http://www.alzheimers.nia.nih.gov
A service of the National Institutes of Health, ADEAR provides information on research and clinical trials.

Alzheimer's Foundation of America
E-mail: info@alzfdn.org
Web site: http://alzfdn.org
The AFA provides outreach to patients with AD and other forms of dementia, as well as their caretakers. The AFA web site provides information on dementia, news about the latest studies, and guidance for caretakers.

Alzheimer's Research Forum
Web site: http://www.alzforum.org
Primarily for researchers studying AD, but non-researchers may find valuable information about the latest findings in the search for a cure.

AlzGene Web site
Web site: http://www.alzgene.org
A site that pinpoints more than a dozen genes related to AD research

Association for Frontotemporal Dementias (AFTD)
E-mail: info@FTD-Picks.or g
Web site: http://www.FTD-Picks.org
AFTD is a non-profit organization dedicated to promoting research and educating the public about frontotemporal

dementias, which often lead to symptoms similar to those of Alzheimer's disease.

John Douglas French Alzheimer's Foundation

E-mail: jdfaf@earthlink.net

Web site: http://www.jdfaf.org

This foundation supports AD research in the state of California. The Web site includes information about some of the latest breakthroughs supported by the foundation.

National Institute of Mental Health (NIMH)

E-mail: nimhinfo@nih.gov

Web site: http://www.nimh.nih.gov

The U.S. government organization dedicated to mental health research

National Hospice and Palliative Care Organization/ National Hospice Foundation

E-mail: Nhpco_info@nhpco.org

Web site: http://www.nhpco.org

A nonprofit outreach organization dedicated to improving end-of-life care to those with terminal illness

Neuroscience for Kids

Web site: http://faculty.washington.edu/chudler/alz.html

A simplified, illustrated overview of Alzheimer's disease geared towards children

PICTURE CREDITS

INDEX

ABOUT THE AUTHOR

Evelyn B. Kelly, Ph.D., is a writer, educator, and community activist living in Ocala, Florida. She specializes in writing about the diseases and disorders of the nervous and endocrine systems and enjoys tackling cutting-edge research. Throughout her years as a writer, she has written more than 400 articles and 12 books, including *The Skeletal System* (2004), *Obesity* (2006), *Stem Cells* (2007), and *Gene Therapy* (2007) for Greenwood Press.

Evelyn is a professor of education at Saint Leo University, Ocala Campus. She teaches classroom organization and management, educational law and ethics, and supervises interns. Evelyn lives on a farm in Ocala with her husband, Charles. She has four children and four grandchildren. Her Ph.D. is in Educational Curriculum and Instruction from the University of Florida. She is an international speaker on educational topics and, as a world traveler, has visited 58 countries and all seven continents.